GURUS ON
STRATEGY

TONY GRUNDY

THOROGOOD

First published by Thorogood 2003
Reprinted 2004

Thorogood
10-12 Rivington Street
London EC2A 3DU

Telephone: 020 7749 4748
Fax: 020 7729 6110
Email: info@thorogood.ws
Web: www.thorogood.ws

A CIP catalogue record for this book is
available from the British Library.

HB: ISBN 1 85418 222 6
PB: ISBN 1 85418 262 5

Cover and book designed by Driftdesign.

Printed in India by Replika Press.

About the author

Dr Tony Grundy is Director of Cambridge Corporate Development and Senior Lecturer in Strategic Management at Cranfield. He is an independent strategy facilitator (contact: 01494 873934 or a.grundy@cranfield.ac.uk).

Contents

List of illustrations   ix

Introduction   1
What have the strategy gurus got to tell us?   1

ONE   **A taster of the gurus**   5
Introduction   5
What is strategy?   5
Understanding the external environment   9
Understanding competitive advantage   15
Strategic options and decision-making   19
Implementation   21
Learning and control   22
Conclusion   22

TWO   **Key strategic concepts**   23
Introduction   23
The key concepts   23

THREE   **The business strategy gurus**   37
Igor Ansoff (a major guru)   40
Chris Argyris   46
Christopher Bartlett and Samantha Ghoshal
(major gurus)   48
G Bennett-Stewart   49
Blackadder   51
Boston Consulting Group   53
Cliff Bowman   55
Braybrooke and Lindblom   58

Campbell A and Goold
(major gurus – despite being in the UK)   60
Alfred Chandler (a major guru)   63
A De Geus   65
Eliyahu Goldratt   67
Robert Grant   69
Tony Grundy (the alternative guru – the author)   71
Gary Hamel and S K Prahalad (major gurus)   77
Charles Handy (a major guru – and from the UK)   80
P Haspeslagh and D Jemison   82
Gerry Johnson and Kevin Scholes (UK gurus)   84
Rosebeth Moss Kanter (a major guru)   86
Kaplan and Norton (major gurus)   88
Kurt Lewin (a major guru – albeit a long time ago)   90
P Lorange and J Roos   91
McTaggart, Kontes and Mankins   92
Henry Mintzberg (a major guru)   94
Ian Mitroff   97
Kenichi Ohmae   101
R T Pascale (a major guru)   103
Tom Peters (a major guru)   105
Nigel Piercy   108
Michael E Porter (a major guru)   110
J B Quinn   116
Alfred Rappaport   119
Peter Senge (a major guru)   123
A Slyvosky   126
J C Spender   128
E Stalk   129
Sun Tzu (a major guru, now deceased)   131
David Ulrich (a major guru)   133
P Wack   135
Jack Welch (a major guru)   137
George Yip   139

FOUR   **Champney's health resort and the**
business strategy gurus   **140**

Introduction   140

Background   141

Strategic analysis   142

Strategic choice   149

Implementation   152

Champney's strategic breakthroughs   158

Implementing the strategic breakthroughs   159

A summary of Champney's strategic
change breakthroughs   164

Key lessons from the Champney's case   165

Champney's – Some options for competitive strategy   166

Organisational strategy – Options   169

Case postscript   171

Conclusion   171

Summary of key points   172

FIVE   **Marks & Spencer and the**
business strategy gurus   **173**

Introduction   173

Marks & Spencer – The position mid-1990s   174

Marks & Spencer – Recipes for success   177

Marks & Spencer – The position 1997 – 2001   183

Marks & Spencer – Turning to the future   190

Conclusion   191

SIX	**Checklists for managing strategy**	**192**
	Introduction	192
	Organic business development strategies	193
	New product strategies	193
	New market strategies	195
	Selling more to existing customers	196
	New value-creating activities	197
	New distribution channel strategies	198
	New technologies	199
	Strategic and financial planning processes	200
	Restructuring strategies	201
	Information systems strategy	202
	Management buy-out strategies	203
	Alliance and joint venture strategies	204
	Setting strategy and objectives	207
	Acquisition evaluation	208
	Negotiating the deal	209
	Integration	210
	Operational strategies	211
	Conclusion	212
SEVEN	**Conclusion – gurus and the future**	**213**
References		**215**

List of illustrations

1	Strategy process	9
2	PEST factors	10
3	Porter's five forces	11
4	Strategic option grid, Grundy 2003	19
5	Ansoff grid	41
6	SWOT analysis	42
7	Gap analysis	44
8	The BCG matrix	53
9	Perceived use value/relative price	54
10	Growth drivers	72
11	The strategy mix	73
12	Deliberate and emergent strategy	95
13	Uncertainty – importance grid	98
14	Kenichi Ohmae's three C's	102
15	Stakeholder analysis grid	108
16	Business value system – football industry	112
17	Value drivers	120
18	Cost drivers	120
19	Value over time curve	122
20	Scenario development	124
21	The uncertainty tunnel	135
22	Octopus	150
23	Force field analysis at Champney's	160
24	Champney's stakeholder analysis	163
25	A brief summary of M&S financial performance 1994 – 1990	176
26	M&S financial performance 1997 – 2002	185

Introduction

What have the strategy gurus got to tell us?

There are a number of reasons why it might be worth knowing about the Strategy Gurus.

- You might just want to be familiar with their names, and a few of the concepts which they have given us.

- You may want to go more deeply into what they have to say, providing a fuller framework for understanding some management issues in the organisation around you.This might extend to having a process for doing strategic thinking yourselves.

- You may wish to expand your learning of leading management thinking, perhaps as a preliminary to doing an MBA.

- And finally, you may be keen to use some Guru concepts more directly and practically on some of your own issues.

This book addresses all of these needs.

10 Key tenets from the Business Strategy Gurus

So, if we were to distil the lessons of the strategy gurus into ten key tenets about strategy, we would find:

1 A strategy is a plan, indeed a cunning plan (Ansoff (1965), Blackadder (1999)).

2 But strategies are often created in, and managed in an incremental way (Quinn).

3 Successful strategies need to be rooted in competitive advantage (Ohmae (1982), Porter (1985)).

4 Strategy often means changing the rules of the game (Hamel and Prahalad (1994)).

5 Some markets are inherently more attractive than others, because of their competitive forces (Porter (1980)).

6 But in many cases these strategies emerge, (and are thus called 'emergent') rather than are 'deliberate'.

7 Regardless of their form, a useful starting point is to Think Future – and how you will compete differently in the future – and then work backwards to define your strategy, or cunning plan (Hamel and Prahalad (1994)).

8 A successful strategy requires the exploration of many options (*Winnie The Pooh, Milne* (1926).

9 And this might entail creating some overall pictures, or stories of the future (Wack (1985)).

10 Imagination in strategy is insufficient, change is also often necessary (Kanter (1983)).

These are some very important and practical lessons which can make a very real difference to how well we manage. In this book we will develop those themes, giving you at the same time an overview of both the major and the minor strategy gurus.

This guide to strategy gurus is structured by topic as follows:

ONE A taster of the gurus

A look at strategy as a management concept, from the gurus' viewpoint and the need for creativity and innovative thanking, not just analysis.

TWO Key strategic concepts

An alphabetical look at the key concepts of strategy from Acquisitions through to Vision and Uncertainty.

THREE A detailed, guru-by-guru guide

An alphabetical listing, from Ansoff to Yip, of the Business Strategy Gurus, the main concepts they are famous for and how they link to each other.

FOUR AND FIVE Two integrative case studies – illustrating the gurus perspectives with checklists for managing strategy

- An in-depth study of Champney's Health Resort and the relevance of the Strategy Gurus
- A detailed look at the considerable management challenges encountered by Marks & Spencer.

SIX Checklists for managing strategy

A selection of useful checklists for managing your strategy in:

- Organic business development,
- Strategic and financial planning,
- Restructuring,
- Management buy-outs,
- Alliances and joint ventures, and
- operational situations.

SEVEN Conclusion – gurus and the future

A look at where we could go from here.

ONE
A taster of the gurus

Introduction

Strategy is a much used, but much misunderstood, concept in manage-ment. In this introductory chapter we therefore begin by using the gurus to answer the question 'What is strategy?' We then look at what the main gurus say on managing the external environment. Our next port of call is the notion of competitive advantage – what is this and why is this impor-tant? This is followed by a section on strategic decision-making.

Another important area is implementation and change management. Many good strategies fail because they are badly implemented and not because they are not robust. In the final phase the monitoring of the strategy needs to be considered, through learning and control.

What is strategy?

Strategy can be defined in a number of ways. The 'design school' strategy theorists, who consider strategy to be a part of a well formed, logical planning process (Ansoff, 1965, Porter 1980, 1985) might define 'strategy' as:

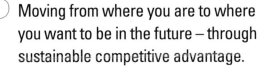

> Moving from where you are to where you want to be in the future – through sustainable competitive advantage.

Strategy can also be defined much more fluidly, perhaps even as 'emergent' strategy. Strategy in this mode is defined by Mintzberg (1994) as:

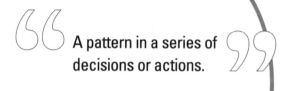

> **A pattern in a series of decisions or actions.**

According to Mintzberg, strategy thus may not be something which is within a formal plan, but is more likely to be discovered intuitively. This can be achieved by reflecting on what has actually already happened, or what is currently happening, or what is about to happen.

Whilst these conceptual definitions are useful (to a point) much of strategic management is hidden behind theoretical language. To demystify the concept let us now look to an unusual source.

A further definition of strategy (which is perhaps more off-the-wall is that drawn from Blackadder (the Television comedy) which is in turn derived from everyday usage). Quite simply, strategy is 'The Cunning Plan.'

A 'cunning plan' is something which has some, or even all of the characteristics of the following:

- Where there is a major constraint, there is some non-obvious way of getting around it

- Where there is a stretching objective, there is a way of getting there in a way which secures maximum advantage, or at minimum cost, or in minimum time

- Is likely to involve looking at the problem or opportunity from a novel and perhaps surprising perspective

- Is fundamentally simple at bottom
- May well incorporate solutions from unrelated areas of experience (e.g. from other industries)

(For more on the 'cunning plan', see the section on 'Blackadder' as a guru in Chapter 3.)

From the not so cunning plan to the 'cunning plan'

For example, when writing this book I visited the British Grand Prix at Silverstone. My son James and I were running late for the Saturday qualifiers. We shot out of our car (without checking our exact location). On our return later that day we came out of what looked like the same exit (but it wasn't). As we had entered our car park from a different angle we could not locate our car – indeed, we were actually looking in the wrong place in a sea of cars.

After fifteen minutes, and getting increasingly desperate, we looked for assistance from one of the stewards, who suggested a not-so-cunning plan:

"You can't find your car?", he said.

"No", I responded.

"What kind of car was it?", he asked.

"It's an Audi A4, dark red", I said.

"What was its registration number?", he then asked.

"N151 SPE", was my response.

Pausing for a moment to reflect, he then said, "Maybe if you walked around you could see if you could spot it."

We rolled our eyes and resumed our long search.... Finally we realised we had come out of a different exit and we found the car. On the journey home, as an amusing piece of in-car entertainment, I got us both to *brainstorm* more cunning plans for how we might have found it. These included:

ELEVEN CUNNING WAYS FOR FINDING OUR CAR

1 Borrowing a very large ladder from Octogan, who run the Grand Prix.

2 Climbing up the mobile phone ariel (adjacent to the car park (with a radioactive – proof suit)).

3 Going on the Big Wheel adjacent to the car park.

4 Asking to take over from one of the cameramen who track the Grand Prix with telescopic cameras mounted on incredibly tall platforms.

5 Climbing on the roof of one of the more central cars – without damaging it.

6 Chartering a helicopter (at £1000 an hour).

7 Parachuting down on the car park (a bit dangerous, though).

8 Waiting until all the cars had gone (perhaps not-so-cunning-this one).

9 Calling in the SAS to home in on our car with laser sights.

10 Contacting the Pentagon to obtain high resolution/magnified pictures of the car park (either by Blackbird spy-plane or by spy-satellite).

11 Bribing the steward £200 to call in his entire team to help us find it (the best one – very simple).

The above example illustrates:

- The need for creative and innovative thinking in developing a strategy and not merely analysis.
- The equal need to be creative in challenging constraints and in acquiring and deploying resources – for competitive advantage.

- The imperative to make trade-offs between options – in coming to a strategic choice, and particularly to assess the implementation difficulty ahead.

- In essence, the best strategies often have the ingredient of SIMPLICITY.

- The importance of understanding the potential for opportunities which may not be self-evident in the external.

We now turn to environment, our final point above – understanding the external environment.

Understanding the external environment

A classic model of the strategy process (which we now work through is contained in Figure 1.

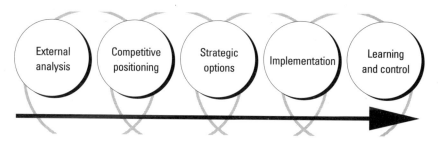

External analysis   Competitive positioning   Strategic options   Implementation   Learning and control

FIGURE 1: STRATEGY PROCESS

The external environment is (and has always been) a major preoccupation of strategy. Ansoff (1965) underlined the need for scanning the wider environment review. Many of the strategy consultants still (today) employ models which have roots in Ansoff.

Ansoff's 'environmental scanning breaks down into 'strong' signals (for example, the onset of a sudden recession) and 'weak' signals (for example, the slowing of growth on demand for letters post in the UK around the turn of the century) due at least in part to the explosion in the use of e-mail.

One of the most under spread models for environmental scanning is 'SWOT' analysis (Ansoff 1965). SWOT analysis (strengths, weaknesses and, more particularly, opportunities and threats analysis) can help to identify external changes with a direct or indirect impact on your business.

Whilst 'SWOT' is an extremely common strategic technique and perhaps the dominant one in most organisations it might be accused of being limited and even dangerous.

Its deficiencies include:

- Inefficiency (Professor Cliff Bowman of Cranfield School of Management jokingly calls this a 'Stupid Waste of Time).
- Subjectivity – especially of its 'strengths'.
- Incompleteness: especially of the 'threats' and also 'weaknesses' listed.
- Inadequate interpretation (what is its so-what?) For example, what is really important in it, and what strategic options does it suggest (Grundy 2003).

Environmental scanning can be done at a variety of levels. For instance, we can consider the PEST factors at large in the environment. At the most general level these begin with the 'PEST' factors (or the Political, Economic, Social and Technological factors) – see Figure 2.

Equally important are the factors driving growth (within the market itself) or 'growth drivers' (see Chapter 2), (see Figure 10). Next, within the market itself, are the five competitive forces (Porter 1980) (see Figure 3).

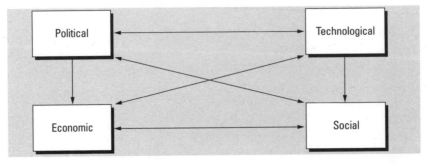

FIGURE 2: PEST FACTORS

After 'SWOT' analysis Porter's five forces is one of the most prominent techniques taught on MBA courses.

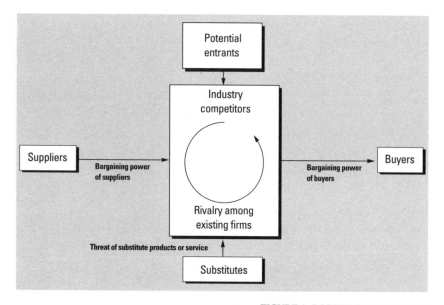

FIGURE 3: PORTER'S FIVE FORCES

It would be remiss to omit mention of futures and scenarios in considering the external environment. A 'scenario' is defined as being:

> A picture or story-line of the future which is internally consistent and insightful.

We'll now look at a typical scenario of an industry.

A scenario for the football premiership – 2002/3

Following Manchester United's disappointing season in 2001/2002, Sir Alex Ferguson agrees the sale of the Argentinean Veron for £25 million and buys Rio Ferdinand Colefence) for £29 million. Its captain, Roy Keane, keen to make amends for his dropping out 'of Ireland's World Cup Challenge, resumes his assertive role at the heart of Manchester United. Its nearest contender, Arsenal, weakened by injuries to its world-class players and due to tiredness drop to number three position. This leaves Manchester United to romp home to yet another double, and come a near-second in the European Champions Cup final.

Scenarios draw from a number of our earlier environmental analysis techniques in their development. In particular they will require thinking about:

- PEST analysis: to explore changes in the wider industry context, and their knock on effect.

- The growth drivers: to consider shifts in those factors driving growth, – in terms of new ones coming in, old ones becoming less influential, or even turning into brakes on growth.

- Porters five forces: to explore changes in the structure and dynamics of the industry (for example from low to high rivalry, from low bargaining power of the buyers to medium bargaining power).

- The industry mind-set: the industry mind-set is defined (Grundy 1994, 2003) as being:

  'The set of perceptions, assumptions and expectations in the industry which determine how key players add value and compete with one another'

  This concept is also implicit in Hamel and Prahalad (1994) who argue that Porter's forces should not be seen as 'givens' but as open to innovation, challenge and to disruptive competitive behaviour. This concept helps us to understand Porter's five forces from a psychological viewpoint – indeed it has been suggested (Grundy 2002) that this could be a competitive force missed by Michael Porter).

According to HSBC's Head of Strategy Development Mike Guest:

"I think there is something missing here in Porter's five forces, we also need to think about the industry mind-set."

"In our industry it is probably the most important competitive force."

In learning about futures more generally, there is nothing better to read than Hamel and Prahalad (1994). In sharp contrast to the majority of the literature on scenarios (what tends to be highly (and unnecessarily) technical and remote) Hamel and Prahalad's thinking is a breath of fresh air. Perhaps for a change we find gurus who are really in touch with the practical issues which managers face, for example:

'How do I think differently about my industry?'

and

'How do I avoid accepting my current competitive advantage as a 'given'?'

For in many markets both market attractiveness and competitive position *are not givens*, but they are asking for someone to change the rules of the game.

For example, in the mid-1990s the author performed a Porter's five forces of the strategy consulting industry. This suggested that:

- The bargaining power of the buyers in the market was 'low' to 'medium'.
- The entry barriers were high (brand is very important – as well as competence and experience.
- Rivalry was low between consulting firms.
- Supplier power was medium/high (to hire someone to be competent in strategy consulting was very expensive due to scarcity of analysis and process skills).
- The threat of substitutes was high (see below).

Focusing on the final force, 'substitutes', I realised that this was a negative force (companies either wanted to do it themselves) or they were so frightened of being 'ripped off' by the strategy consulting firms that they would either try to do it themselves, or maybe even not do it at all (properly).

This gave me a rather important and profound set of insights, namely:

1 'Substitutes' was the force I had to work on – and not the others.

2 The business I was in (being a strategy consultant) could be redefined as 'Avoiding Strategy Consultants' – so I train them to do it themselves.

3 If I was able to help major companies to avoid strategy consultants – with more value, at less cost and in less time, then I would have Porter's elusive 'sustainable competitive advantage'.

4 This would be easy for me and difficult for the big strategy firms because:

   a) they would need to shoot themselves in the foot to compete with me and

   b) they couldn't possibly compete with me because they sell in terms of teams and weeks (their mind-set), whilst I sold in terms of myself (and days).

Quick example

Another quick example of the use of scenarios and of futures was that of a major retailer who, in the mid/late 1990s was contemplating entering the homeshopping market. At that time they had limited market presence on that emerging market.

Their (independent) consultant said to them:

"I am not sure that competing from where we are now is going to be particularly helpful. Why don't we simply imagine the market in 2002?"

The team looked at their future homeshopping market – which seemed in (post-Internet) to be substantial and potentially profitable – and thus interesting. They said to their consultant: "This is a pretty big and attractive market given the PEST factors, the growth drivers, and the competitive forces."

Their consultant then said: "Well, where do *you* want to be in it?"

Their response was, "Well, given that we are Bestco, we want to be dominant in it."

"So that is your starting point", said their consultant (and the rest was history).

Understanding competitive advantage

Besides analysis of the external environment the next major thing we learn from the gurus is to analyse and evolve our competitive advantage.

'Competitive advantage' was defined by Kenichi Ohmae, head of strategy, McKinsey Co, Tokyo as being:

EITHER

" Delivering superior value advantage to your target customers relative to your competitors "

OR

" Delivering equivalent customer value to your target customers relative to your competitors but at lower cost "

Kenichi Ohmae's book 'The Mind of the Strategist' (1982) is short, brilliant in style, and succinct. It is an extremely lucid and relevant account of the basis of competitive strategy.

Somewhat more heavyweight is Porter's 'Competitive Advantage' (1985). The book was published during the last year of my MBA in 1985. It represented a major advance in thinking about strategy. Already, in 1980, Porter had put himself both globally and eternally on the map with his thoughtful and well researched book on 'Competitive Strategy'. This was centred on:

- His five competitive forces (see Figure 3) and
- Applying life-cycle analysis not just to products/markets, but to entire industries (and many of his insights are just as relevant today).

'Competitive Strategy' is superbly structured taking the reader through the evolution of markets, and examining how the five competitive forces change over the industry life-cycle.

'Competitive Advantage' (of 1985 vintage) was perhaps more of a break-through in jargon than one of intellectual advance. It was a superbly packaged book. Instead of thinking about SWOT analysis, we were now encouraged to think about securing an incremental competitive advantage, over and above that of our competitors.

The idea of 'competitive advantage' already existed implicitly in economics but, Porter's brilliance here was to turn an essentially economic idea into one which was an every day, catchy, management notion. And this certainly caught on. Every business school in the world jumped on the (then) bandwagon of 'competitive advantage'.

Possibly the strategy world has never seen anything like this level of excitement since. Indeed since that time there have been a lot of confusions about Porters notion of 'generic competitive advantages'. These were perhaps motivated in part by genuine mistrust of generic prescriptions but also, perhaps to be just a little tinge of academic rivalry.

Surprisingly, since 1985 Porter appears to have regarded his work on competitive strategy as more or less finished at least at the business/corporate strategy level) and has moved onto 'better things' (looking at countries as quasi strategic business units).

Many have critiqued his work, few have built from it. Whilst Porter brought together perhaps the first, truly comprehensive and detailed account of the analytical needs for developing a competitive strategy, it is a pity that so few have sought to refine his ideas further.

MBA students who have relied to so far only on secondary texts of Porter's work (some examples are Johnson and Scholes (1989) or Grundy (1994, 2002)) would do well to avoid being lazy and to read Porter in the original.

Turning back now to Porter's more controversial, second work 'Competitive Advantage', the more novel areas of this book are:

- The suggestions that these are a number of 'generic' strategies (or ideal forces of strategy), including 'differentiation' (or high value-added strategy) 'costs leadership' (having the lowest costs) or 'focus' (competing on a narrower area).

- The prescription that if you do not make a strategic choice and if you try to pursue a number of different generic strategies simultaneously then you will lose focus within your strategy, and this will undermine your strategic success.

The key reasons why there is likely to be tension within an organisation pursuing differentiation *and* cost leadership styles of strategy simultaneously include:

- The customer might get confused with contradictory brand messages.

- Common processes may result in it being difficult to cope with the opposing demands of these polar, strategy styles.

- The organisational culture and mind-set is unlikely to be able to cope with the imperative to switch styles of competing, depending upon what product market is being serviced at that particular moment in time.

To get around this limitation companies might try to 'have it both ways' nevertheless, for example by:

- Offering superior value for money – with the trade off being that there is a more limited product offering, thus gaining economies of scale over a smaller volume (Marks and Spencers clothing strategy 1990-1997).

- Creating a back office for commodity-type activities, whilst attempting to differentiate through the brand, the core product, and through sales process (this was the UK bank, Abbey National's strategy). However, this strategy can prove difficult to sustain where the customers are affected by quality problems in obtaining routine servicing from the back office.

- Having decentralised business units who do not need to get confused by conflicting mind-sets. (For example, British Airways set up the budget airline 'Go' to compete with EasyJet in the late 1990s. But this proved hard to sustain – both because of competitive conditions and the difficulties of reporting to a corporate parent with a different mind-set. Go was then bought out and subsequently EasyJet bid to become its new corporate parent company in 2002.)

Looking back at Porter's book on 'Competitive Advantage' – which was, and is still now – a very helpful concept – one cannot help feeling that its battle-cry might (inadvertently) have sometimes led to an inappropriate mind-set. For although companies pursue competitive advantage they are often motivated to excel in some areas, this is frequently done to the detriment of others. In many ways an even more pertinent concept is that of:

Avoiding competitive disadvantage

…for so many companies fail to grow a sustainable competitive advantage not because they are not able to differentiate or achieve low cost positions, but because they undermine the effective delivery of customer value.

Short case study – Einstein Finance

'Einstein Finance' was a new and innovative financial services provider which aimed to give extra value for money to the customer by excellent deposit rates, innovative style accounts, and customer service by bright call centre staff. It invested heavily in television and other advertising, its name suggesting that it was a really clever place to put ones money.

One of its customers invested one hundred pounds with Einstein Finance. He was intending to invest a further £60,000 following a property sale.

Unfortunately on his first telephone enquiry it took twenty minutes to get an answer.

This went as follows:

"Thank you for your patience, we value your call, please listen to this pleasant music to prevent you from getting bored…", said the electronic voice.

"Einstein Finance", the (human) teleoperator then said (eventually).

"Thank you for answering at last, but I have now passed the ultimate intelligence test and wish to withdraw all my money forthwith", said the author.

Strategic options and decision-making

One of the central notions of strategy is 'choice' (Porter 1985). This means choice of positioning and also effective allocation of resources (Grant 1991). Choice means being able to apply decision criteria in a multitude of strategic settings, including deliberate and emergent strategies.

The criteria for strategic decision-making are dispersed throughout many strategy books, with tests of 'sustainability', 'feasibility' or 'fit' often being used. To cut through this mist of often very general criteria, it is proposed to the reader that Figure 4 below is very much worth a try.

Options / Criteria	Option 1	Option 2	Option 3	Option 4
Strategic attractiveness				
Financial attractiveness*				
Implementation difficulty				
Uncertainty and risk				
Acceptability (to stakeholders)				

Benefits less costs – net cash flows relative to investment

FIGURE 4: STRATEGIC OPTION GRID, GRUNDY 2003

Besides looking to the academic gurus we should also look at who are leading the way in terms of applying strategic analysis tools in dealing with ambiguous, uncertain and even intractable decisions. A number of major companies have now used/are adopting this technique, for example:

- Diageo
- Ford
- HSBC
- Microsoft
- Nokia
- Standard Life
- Tesco

The five criteria on the strategic option grid can be scored using:

✔✔✔ very attractive

✔✔ moderately attractive

✔ less attractive

These scores are then added up at the bottom to see what is (prima facie) the most attractive option.

Note that if something is 'very difficult' it is scored as a one tick and not a three – likewise with 'high uncertainty and risk'.

These scores are only as good as 'the cunning plan' – implying a high degree of creativity rather than merely analysis. Once the scores have a preliminary estimate, you should then check them out with bottom-up techniques (as follows), and with carefully selected data analysis:

Strategic attractiveness	PEST factors, Porter's five forces, growth drivers (Grundy/Ohmaes/Porter's competitive advantage)
Financial attractiveness	Value and cost drivers (see shareholder value theory later in the book)
Implementation difficulty	Force field analysis (Lewin)

| Uncertainty and risk | Key assumptions (Mitroff) |
| Stakeholder acceptability | Stakeholder positionings (Piercy) |

Whilst the gurus describe strategic decision-making as being typically emergent, (Mintzberg 1994) messy (Braybrooke and Lindblom (1963) and incremental (Quinn 1980), using the strategic option grid gives at least some clarity to senior managers in future direction. In practice strategy tends to move through different states of degree of form and logic, as we will see in the section in Chapter 3 on Grundy – 'The Strategy Mix' (Figure 11).

Effectively, the Strategic Option Grid (Grundy 2002) therefore brings together (in practical terms) the disparate insights of a variety of gurus.

Implementation

Whilst the design school (Ansoff, Porter, Hamel and Prahalad) tend to focus on deliberate external strategy, process theorists tend to focus on emergent strategy and on organisational factors. It is this rare to find rounded accounts of implementation in the strategy literature (except perhaps for Johnson and Scholes, 1987).

As the book develops we will see the need to draw from the more behavioural work of theorists like Peters (1982), Kanter (1983) and Pascale (1990), some analytical techniques, notably:

- Force field analysis (Lewin 1935).
- Stakeholder analysis (Piercy 1989).

These are essential techniques to anticipate, and to avoid, implementation difficulty.

Learning and control

The literature on learning and control is quite patchy – apart from the Balanced Score-Card (Kaplan and Norton, 1991) and the emphasis on the learning organisation (Senge 1990). One of the major limitations on organisations in this area is not so much process mechanisms, but an absence of strategic leadership (contrast later on our Champney's case, Chapter 4, with Marks and Spencers, Chapter 5.

Conclusion

Whilst strategic theory is well developed in terms of external analysis there are far less well developed frameworks of strategy implementation, learning and control. The organisational literature (as would find) tends either not to be too helpful as it just accepts what is – however bad, or it is dominated by prescriptive gurus like Peters. This gives pointers for new avenues of strategy and guru development for the future.

TWO
Key strategic concepts

Introduction

In this chapter we now define the key concepts of strategy, link them to each other and also the main gurus as sources.

The key concepts

Acquisitions

Acquisitions involve one company having a controlling interest in another one. Acquisitions can be characterised as 'in-fill' versus 'step-out', 'related' or 'inter-related' (Haspeslagh and Jemison 1991; Grundy 2002). (Linked concept to alliances, mergers, integration.)

Alliances

An alliance is a longer-term partnership between two or more organisations. Alliances can be relatively loose and tactical through to 'strategic'. A strategic alliance involves a reciprocal commitment by the various parties to longer-term collaboration which involves the mutual deployment of resources. These resources could involve money, time and attention. These resources may be supplied to a specific venture (perhaps structured as a company), or on an on-going basis. (Linked concept to acquisitions.)

Benchmarking

Benchmarking involves some comparison of performance and of some underlying capability – in order to achieve learning and change. Customer benchmarking entails comparison of customer needs against supplier delivery (Ohmae 1982). Competitive benchmarking involves understanding differences between delivery of value to customers, or cost (or both) between at least two players (Grundy 2002). World-class benchmarking involves comparison with the best in the world, either within or outside your industry. Internal benchmarking looks at the learnings from comparison of different operations within your ownership. Cyclical benchmarking looks at performance levels either between economic cycles or over an entire cycle. (Linked concept to competitive advantage.)

Buyer power

This is the degree of pressure which buyers have over companies in terms of price, discounts, delivery times, quality levels and penalties for poor quality. Buyer power will vary by market, segment, distribution channel and customer. It will also vary according to whether it is a primary supply or a secondary supply (e.g. spares – in the latter case buyer power is usually lower) (Porter 1980). (Linked concept to Porter's five forces.)

Breakthrough

A breakthrough is a major shift in a company's competitive position, organisational capability and financial performance (or all three) (Grundy 1994, 2002). (Linked concept to gap analysis.)

Capability

This is the overall ability of a company to compete (Ulrich and Lake 1990). (Linked concept to competencies and HR strategy.)

Competitive advantage

This is about either adding superior value to your target customers or similar value at lower cost (relative to your competitors). (Linked concept to capability, resource based theory, imitability.) (Porter 1985.)

Core competence

A core competence is a particular skill area which a company has which will enable it to add value to its customers, and to manage its cost base. An example of a core competence is Virgin Group's expertise in brand development (Hamel and Prahalad 1994). (Linked concept to capability, resource based theory.)

Competitive positioning

This is a distinctive way of competing (Porter 1985). (Linked concept to generic strategies.)

Competitive strategy

The scope of what business you are in, the relative focus on differentiation, focus on cost leadership strategy, and the resources and competencies used to deliver that generic strategy (Porter 1985; Hamel and Prahalad 1994). (Sometimes called 'business strategy' – linked concept to corporate strategy.)

Competitive rivalry

The extent of competition between existing rivals within an industry (Porter 1980). (Linked concept to Porter's five forces.)

Corporate strategy

This is the scope of existing businesses which a group is in, the intended future businesses (and the strategy to develop them) and the way in which the corporate centre adds value to them. (Ansoff 1965; Campbell and Goold 1994; Porter 1987).

Cost drivers

The direct or indirect factors both within and outside the business, now and in the future, which generates cash outflows (Grundy 2002; Rappaport 1986). (Linked concept to value drivers.)

Cost leadership

This is a strategy which aims to achieve the lowest unit costs either within an industry or within a particular strategic group (or grouping of like-minded and similar competitors) (Porter 1980). (Linked concept to differentiation, focus strategies.)

Cost of capital

This is the level of financial return required to achieve minimal satisfaction of suppliers of capital (both from shares – 'risk capital', long-term loans and other methods of longer-term financing) (McTaggart et al. 1994; Rappaport 1986; Reimann 1990). (Linked concept to shareholder value.)

Culture

This is the set of characteristic values, attitudes and behaviours which are characteristic of an organisation, or of a part of it (Kanter 1983; Pascale 1990; Peters and Waterman 1982). (Linked concept to style, strategic leadership, paradigms and values.)

Deliberate strategy

This is a strategy which takes detailed account of a) market attractiveness, b) competitive position, and c) changes in the markets and in customers needs and d) competitor intent, (Ansoff 1965; Mintzberg 1994; Porter 1985). (Linked concept to emergent strategy, strategic intent.)

De-merger

This is the unbundling of a business, or of a group of businesses, into stand-alone units. This unbundling splits up these into groupings with differing growth, competitive strategies, industry sectors, future potential, prospects, financial performance, and perceived attractiveness to shareholders (Campbell and Goold 1994).

Differentiation

This is a generic strategy, aimed at generating either more real or perceived value to its target customers than its competitors. (Linked concept to cost leadership, focus strategies) (Porter, 1985.)

Diversification

This is a shift into either new products, new markets, new channels to market, new technologies, now geographic domains or into new competencies (or into a combination of some of these) (Ansoff 1965; Porter 1987). (Linked concept to gap analysis.)

Divestment

This is a decision to sell, close or automatically downscale an operation (Campbell and Goold 1994).

Dominance

This is a competitive position which is so strong a player has either the controlling market share, the number one brand, unique access to superior resources or technology, the lowest unit costs (by far), the standard setter, or leadership of industry mindset (or a combination of these things) (Sun Tzu). (Linked concept to sustainable competitive advantage.)

Emergent strategy

This is a pattern in a series of strategic actions or decisions (Mintzberg 1994). (Linked concept to deliberate strategy.)

Entry barriers

Entry barriers are the perceived and real costs, difficulty and risks of entering a particular market. Entry barriers might relate a) to entirely new market entry, or to entry into a new geographic market (by an existing player) (Porter 1980). (Linked concept to Porter's five forces).

Exit barriers

Exit barriers and the perceived costs, difficulty and risks of exiting a particular market (Porter 1980). (Linked concept to Porters five forces).

Financial strategy

This is the sourcing and deployment of sources of capital to get the best balance between cost, risk and return. (Linked concept to shareholder value) (Rappaport 1986.)

Focus strategy

A focus strategy is a generic strategy which is deliberately limited in its scope of markets, products, or technologies (and some or all of these) (Porter 1985). (Linked concept to differentiation and cost leadership.)

Gap analysis

This is the difference between a company's goals and its likely performance given current strategies (Ansoff 1965). (Linked concept to breakthroughs, diversification.)

GE (or General Electric Grid – sometimes called the Directional Policy Matrix)

This is the trade off between inherent market attractiveness (based on growth drivers and Porter's five competitive forces) and the relative competitive position of either a group or of an individual strategic business unit. (Linked concept to positioning.)

Generic strategy

This is a particular style of competing involving the company choosing not only how it *will* compete, but also of how it *will not* compete. Differentiation, cost leadership and focus strategies are all examples of generic strategies (Porter 1985). (Linked concept to competitive advantage.)

Governance

Why do organisations exist and how can their strategies be regulated? This brings in ethical concerns as highlighted by Handy (1989, 1994).

Global strategy

A global strategy is a strategy which deals with strategic issues across national borders, and cultures. By 'global' we do not necessarily mean 'everywhere' or necessarily 'everything'. A global strategy may well focus just on a sub-set of issues, including: market, product development, technology, distribution, organisation, finance, acquisitions and alliances (Bartlett and Ghoshal 1984; Yip 1992).

Growth driver/brakes

A 'growth driver' is any external factor which might either increase volumes sold, or prices – over a particular time period in a market. A 'growth brake' is any external factor which might either decrease volumes sold, or prices – again over a particular time period in a market. (Grundy 2002) (Linked concept to Porter's five forces, PEST analysis.)

HR strategy

An HR strategy is a set of intentions, priorities and plans which aim to shift the capability of an organisation over time to meet present and new challenges (Ulrich and Lake 1990, Grundy 2003, forthcoming). (Linked concept to capability.)

Imitability

Imitability is the relative ease with which competitors or new entrants can imitate a particular company strategy. (This is closely coupled with sustainability – Grant 1991, Porter 1985.) (Linked concept to competitive advantage.)

Industry mind-set

The industry mind-set is the set of perceptions, expectations and assumptions prevalent in a particular industry (Grundy 1994, 2002). (Linked concept to Porter's five forces.)

Integration

Integration is the process of adding value to an acquisition either through absorption, change or development (Haspeslagh and Jemison 1991). (Linked concept to acquisitions.)

Legacy

The legacy of a strategy is the sum of issues from the past. These issues will include the existing resource base and skills, and past strategic decisions (both their successes and failures).

Logical incrementalism

This is the relatively haphazard process through which strategic decisions are made – largely as add-ons, or changes, or deletions to current strategies. Logical incrementalism is to be contrasted with more visionary strategies (Quinn 1980).

Marketing strategy

A marketing strategy is a coherent plan for how to compete in a number of markets, with a clear definition of priorities and with targeted market and financial goals.

Mergers

Mergers involve two businesses or groups coming together on a more-or-less equal footing. (Having said that, many 'mergers' are pretend mergers – they clearly involve one company and one set of managers taking over another one) (Haspeslagh and Jemison 1991). (Linked concept to acquisitions.)

Mission

A 'mission' is a concise and memorable statement of the purpose of why we are in business and of what business we entered into, and how we are going to compete distinctively in them. It should also be inspirational. (Linked concept to vision, strategic leadership.) (Campbell and Goold 1994.)

Many mission statements do not actually pass the above test, being either too long, or too generic (and little more than motherhood statements). In fact many mission statements can actually dilute competitive strategy, and even destroy shareholder value by encouraging the coverage of markets of dubious attractiveness and where there is little real, shareholder value (Campbell 1994). (Linked concept to strategic intent, vision.)

PEST factors

These are the political (and regulatory), economic, social and technological forces impacting on its wider environment (Ansoff 1965). (Linked concept to growth drivers.)

Paradigms

A 'paradigm' is how we do things around here. It is a very close, if not identical concept to culture (Johnson and Scholes 1987). (Linked concept to strategic change, culture, values.)

Positioning

A 'positioning' is the external and internal commitment to serve a particular product/market segment and to compete in a certain way. Positioning implies strategic choice – by taking one strategic position you are implicitly not (at least at present) taking other possible positionings. (Linked concept to emergent strategy.)

Process school

This is the school of strategic thought which regards process as far more important than the analytical content of strategy – and also of analytical techniques (Mintzberg 1994).

Options

The range of alternative strategies or ways of implementing them *(Winnie the Pooh, Milne 1926 – which encourages one to avoid doing the same thing over and over again (like bumping ones head going downstairs, over and over again)).*

Resource-based competitive advantage

The extent to which competitive advantage is based on access to unique or distinctive resources – and which are hard to acquire/imitate (Grant 1991).

Scenarios

A 'scenario' is an internally consistent storyline or picture of the future (De Geus 1988, Wack 1985). (Linked concept to transitional events, uncertainty.)

Shared values

These are the deeply held rules guiding behaviour which are shared through all or part of the organisation (Peters and Waterman 1982).

Shareholder value

This is the perceived or real value of the future discounted cash flows likely to arise from the sum of the business strategies of a group, less the costs of head office. By 'perceived' we mean perceived by the shareholders (as measured by stock market valuation). By 'real' we mean the internal economic value of these strategies, and of their future potential. Besides the existing business strategies of a group we also need to include its opportunity stream, which also has a value (Rappaport 1990; Reimann 1990; McTaggart et al. 1994). (Linked concept to financial strategy.)

Stakeholders

A 'stakeholder' is anyone (internal or external to the business) who is either a decision-maker, adviser, implementer, or victim of the strategy (Piercy 1989, Grundy 2002).

Strategic assumptions

These are the explicit and implicit expectations about the state of the market or of the future success of a company's strategy (Mitroff 1993). (Linked concept to scenarios, assumptions).

Strategic business unit (or SBU)

This is a part of the organisation which is focused specifically on serving a particular product market area – and has the dedicated resources and structure to serve it. SBU's were a concept which came into vogue in the 1960's and 1970's.

Strategic change

This is the incremental or more radical adjustments of a company's competitive strategy and organisations to react to, anticipate and to pre-empt external changes (Johnson and Scholes 1987; Kanter 1983).

Strategic fit

This is the extent to which a new strategy is consistent with, and adds value to overall objectives and intent and to other strategies (Johnson and Scholes 1987).

Strategic intent

The desires, decisions and initial development of resources to achieve particular strategic goals (Hamel 1994). (Linked concept to vision, deliberate strategy.)

Strategic leadership

This is the symbolic embodiment of the strategy in the attitudes, beliefs, behaviours and statements of the Chief Executive and/or his top team (Kanter 1983; Peters 1982). (Linked concept to mission, vision.)

Strategic management

The process of scanning the environment, identifying and prioritising options, resource mobilisation and implementation to pro-actively shape the environment *and to create sustainable competitive advantage* (Ansoff 1963; Porter 1985).

Structure

The organisational framework for channelling the people resource to deliver the strategy without excessive cost, complexity, and time. (Chandler.)

Style

The *way* in which the organisation is actually run, e.g. participative, autocratic etc. (Campbell and Goold 1987; Peters 1982.)

Substitutes

These are the other ways of satisfying customer needs as perceived from a buyer's point of view (Porter 1980).

Supplier power

This is the extent of negotiating power of suppliers to the industry (Porter 1980).

Sustainability

Sustainability can be applied to either growth drivers, the level of competitive pressure generally (Porter's five forces) or to a company's own competitive position. It is the extent to which a strategic situation can be perpetuated without undue cost, difficulty or threat (Porter 1985).

Synergy

This is the creation of incremental value through the sum (whether at the business or corporate level) being more than its parts (Campbell and Goold 1994).

Time-based competitive advantage

This is the potential for a company to gain a competitive edge by speed – either through being able to explicit strategic opportunity faster than competitors (externally), to implement strategic change more quickly or to be able to respond to changing customer needs distinctively quickly (Stalk 1990).

Transitional event

This is an external or internal event what takes either the company or its environment into a new competitive world. (This concept is used in scenario development.)

Value creation

This is the potential of a business strategy, decision or project to generate incremental cash flow in the future to exceed the cost of capital (Grundy 1998; McTaggart et al, Rappaport 1986).

Value destruction

This is the potential for a strategic decision or business unit to produce future negative cash flows or positive ones which are not adequate to cover the cost of capital (Grundy 1998b). (Linked concept to value creation, value dilution, shareholder value.)

Value dilution

This is the potential for the above to make some (accounting, profit) but actually not meet the cost of capital fully (Grundy 1998b). (Linked concept to value creation, value destruction, shareholder value.)

Value drivers

These are direct or indirect factors both within and outside the business, now and in the future, which generate cash in-flows (Grundy 1998b, 2002, 2000e, Rappaport 1986). (Linked concept to cost drivers.)

Values

These are the underlying preferences and rules which guide organisational behaviour (Johnson and Scholes 1987; Kanter 1983; Peters 1982). (Linked concept to culture, paradigms.)

Vision

This is a picture of the future which is either of the market or of ones own position or intent. (Linked concept to strategic leadership, mission, strategic intent.(Peters 1982))

Uncertainty

This is a hard to quantify risk. (Linked concept to scenarios, strategic assumptions(Mitroff 1993.))

THREE
The business strategy gurus

These are our gurus in alphabetical order, and the main things which they are famous for:

Ansoff	corporate planning, diversification, deliberate strategy, environmental scanning
Argyris	strategy and learning
Bartlett and Ghoshal	global competition
Bennett-Stewart	EVA (economic value added)
Blackadder	the cunning plan
Boston Consultancy Group	the BCG matrix
Bowman	Perceived use value/relative price
Braybrooke and Lindblom	strategy as muddling through Boston Consulting Group – the BCG matrix
Campbell and Goold	strategy and styles, the role of the centre
Chandler	strategy and structure
De Geus	scenarios
Goldratt	the theory of constraints
Grant	the resource-based theory (of competitive advantage)
Grundy ('the alternative guru')	strategy and shareholder balance, breakthrough thinking, strategy implementation, HR strategy, strategic behaviour, valuing strategic thinking, acquisitions, HR strategy etc

Hamel and Prahalad	case competencies, strategy as stretch, compelling for the future
Handy	the virtual organisation
Haspeslagh and Jemison	strategic management of acquisitions
Johnson and Scholes	the strategy process (and paradigms)
Kanter	strategic change and catalysts
Kaplan and Norton	the balance score-card
Lewin	force field analysis, organisational resistances
Lorange and Roos	strategic alliances
McTaggart, Kontes & Mankins	shareholder value
Mintzberg	strategic behaviour, organisational forms, emergent strategy
Mitroff	uncertainty analysis
Ohmae	competitive positioning
Pascale	contention in strategy, the seven 's' model
Peters	the seven 'S' model, organisational challenge
Piercy	stakeholder analysis
Porter	Porter's five forces, the generic strategies, industry dynamics, the value chain
Quinn	logical incrementalism (within strategic decision-making)
Rappaport	shareholder value
Senge	the learning organisation
Slyvosky	value migration
Spender	strategic recipes (for decision-making)
Stalk	time-based competition
Sun Tzu	strategies and dominance

Ulrich	organisation capability and competing from within
Wack	scenarios
Welch	organisational transformation
Yip	global strategies

Igor Ansoff (a major guru)

Who is Igor Ansoff?

Igor Ansoff was the founding father of corporate planning. His involvement in Strategic Management extends over several decades. He is to Strategic Management what Mick Jagger of the Rolling Stones was to rock music – and over a similar time scale (from the 60's through to 2000). Igor is a key figure in the school of strategy which extols a more logical, and deliberate approach strategy.

What was he famous for?

Igor was famous for several major things, notably:

- establishing corporate planning as a formal management process.

- popularising SWOT analysis.

- providing us with the Ansoff grid (see Figure 5, page 38) which helps us to understand the degree of risk involved in diversification strategies.

- developing the idea of environmental scanning – and of detecting weak signals – of disruptive environmental change.

- repositioning 'strategic planning' as 'strategic management' i.e. as part of a continuing process rather than a once-a-year (or less frequent) planning process.

- doing battle with Henry Mintzberg on the various advantages and disadvantages of deliberate strategy versus emergent strategy.

- 'Gap' analysis – which looks at the gap between your aspirations and the likely outcome of current strategies.

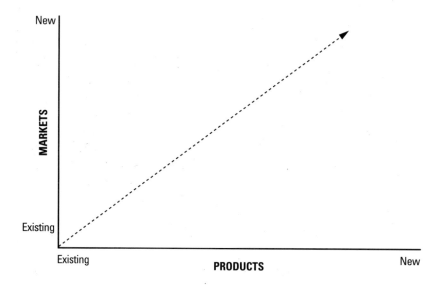

FIGURE 5: ANSOFF GRID

We now look briefly at each of these areas in turn.

Establishing corporate planning as a formal management process

Ansoff's seminal book 'Corporate Planning' emphasised the need to break down the strategy process into a series of steps, distinguishing in particular:

- external analysis – understanding market opportunities and threats.
- internal analysis – understanding strengths and weaknesses.
- choice (and our alternatives).
- implementation.

This model (with refinements) is still used by major strategy consulting firms today (see Figure 1 for a refinement of this).

Popularising SWOT analysis

Whilst it is unclear what the precise origins of SWOT analysis were, it is far clearer that Ansoff's popularisation of this technique not only made it the most commonly used strategic analysis technique over four decades, but also an essential marketing analysis technique. (See Figure 6).

STRENGTHS	**WEAKNESSES**
OPPORTUNITIES	**THREATS**

FIGURE 6: SWOT ANALYSIS

The Ansoff Grid: this grid was one of the key early strategy grids. Its virtue is its simplicity: it compares business development across existing versus new products against existing versus new markets: its core hypothesis is that:

'Development into both new products and new markets simultaneously increases risk substantially and disproportionately.'

Whilst being a cautionary warning, the extensive research on relative success of diversification indicates, perhaps surprisingly, that diversification of this kind does not necessarily reduce performance – *provided that the company is exploiting its core competencies.* Diversification, therefore, is not necessarily a fatal move – indeed to an extent *some degree of diversification is positively associated with superior performance.* The essential proviso here is that the company is innovative – and in a relevant way to its markets.

Repositioning 'strategic planning' as 'strategic management'

Igor took the innovative step of redefining 'strategic planning' as 'strategic management' in order to signify that:

- strategy is not something that one does simply to fall within an annual planning cycle, but as a continuous, ongoing process.
- strategy is not just about responding to environmental change, but should involve *creating a more favourable, competitive environment.*

Environmental scanning

Igor majored on the need to keep an ongoing track of environmental change. In particular, he emphasised the need to be sensitive to 'weak signals' in the environment, for example, signals that you are entering a new economic/competitive era.

Often Ansoff's weak signals are anything but weak. September 11 was a signal – and not such a very weak one – to be prepared for major global disruption on a scale not seen since the Cuban Missile crisis (which threatened World War III) in the 1960s.

The 'deliberate' versus the 'emergent' school of strategy in the early 1990s Igor did battle with Henry Mintzberg over the various merits/demerits of having a deliberate 'versus an emergent' strategy. The long battle in various academic journals ended with about a 4-4 draw with both sides failing to vision the argument discursives. Reading these diatribes one cannot help feeling that this was essentially an artificial disagreement – and that one should draw from both schools of thought, probably equally – in deciding how to manage, strategically.

Gap Analysis

Gap analysis (see Figure 7) is one of the most fundamental – and most forgotten techniques of strategic management – Figure 7 shows:

- Future performance given a 'do nothing' state of the business.
- Future performance – given current plans.
- Future objectives (or Hamel and Prahalad's 'strategy as stretch' (1993)).

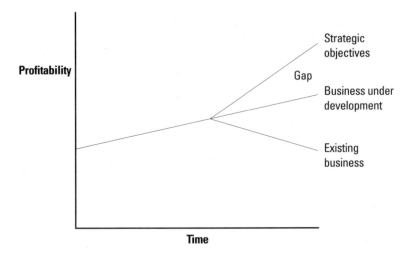

Profitability

Strategic
objectives

Gap

Business under
development

Existing
business

Time

FIGURE 7: GAP ANALYSIS

The central issue to focus on here is that new (breakthrough) strategies should be created to fill the gap whilst gap analysis is an essential feature of any robust strategic plan it does have some drawbacks. The disadvantages of gap analysis are that:

- It can provoke panic to find things to throw into the gap – unless managers have a grounding in how to be strategically creative and also in how to appraise these potential breakthroughs.

- It can limit managers' aspirations – to those objectives dictated by medium-term financial objectives, rather than by the art of the possible (as per Hamel and Prahalad (1994) who we expand on later).

Surprising, Ansoff's gap analysis has virtually dropped out of the mainstream corporate strategy literature and is probably only used by about twenty per cent of companies in practice. The few people who have come across it appear to be marketeers, who have learnt about it through their marketing courses.

The author wonders how major (and more modest) corporations actually develop plans without using gap analysis. (The reality is that it would appear that many plans are mere pretences – as the gap to just hidden in half-grounded forecasts). Probably what actually occurs is that when performance droops top management recover at least some of the gap, albeit temporarily, by Beating Managers Up, i.e. by putting more pressure on them to perform during the annual operating cycle or by reducing cost budgets.

What are his links with other gurus?

As mentioned above, Ansoff is diametrically opposed to Mintzberg in his approach to strategic management. He is very much of the design school, which includes Porter and others.

What are his main works?

1   'Corporate Strategy', New York, McGraw Hill, 1965 – the first complete analytical system of corporate planning.

2   'Managing Surprise by Response to Weak Signals', California Management Review (XVIII 1975) – environment analysis.

3   'The New Corporate Strategy', New York, Wiley 1988 – from strategic planning to strategic management.

What are his key concepts?

- Corporate strategy;
- diversification;
- PEST factors;
- SWOT analysis;
- options;
- strategy process.

Ease of reading – medium.

Chris Argyris

Who is Chris Argyris?

Chris Argyris is a social psychologist by training, and was drawn to strategy through his interest in management behaviour in teams – and also learning in teams. Chris is Professor of organisational behaviour at Harvard University.

Chris has focused (over several decades) on how individuals respond to changing organisational situations and how organisational learning becomes the basis for diagnosis and action.

What was he famous for?

Chris highlighted the importance of learning in teams – and of its antithesis, defensive behaviour. Chris found that the cleverer the team was, the more difficult it became to maintain openness to learning, and to avoid becoming defensive.

He described the process involved here as 'double-loop learning'. Whilst 'single-loop learning' involved doing existing things better, 'double-loop' learning entailed doing existing things in new ways or inventing new things. Effectively, double-loop learning involves reframing problems and stopping outside of existing mind-sets.

The concept of 'double-loop' learning does sound a little bit technical and mysterious, indeed Argyris' language is sometimes hard to understand, perhaps in part to make his ideas appear more profound. Unfortunately this has made him a more esoteric rather than widely known guru, as the essence of his ideas is very significant.

Chris is at his best in the Harvard Business Review when he highlights that where managers are bright they will typically be more averse to making mistakes. Where they do make errors they may well deny them, or react defensively. Argyris calls this (in its most severe form) 'self-sealing errors' so that once errors are made they are covered up (witness the collapse of Enron and Worldcom in 2002).

What are his links with the other gurus?

Argyris' concern with 'strategy as learning' places him close to Senge (1992), who wrote about 'The Learning Organisation'. More of the process school, he provides a good account of the cognitive and political forces which shape emergent/incremental strategies.

What are his main works?

1   'Organizational Learning – A Theory of Action Perspective', Reading, MA, Addison-Wesley 1978) with Schon D.A.

2   'Teaching Smart People How to Learn', Harvard Business Review 69, 3, pp 99-109 May-June 1991.

What are his main concepts?

- Single versus double loop learning;
- defensive routine.

Ease of reading – difficult.

Christopher Bartlett and Samantha Ghoshal (major gurus)

Who are Bartlett and Ghoshal?

Bartlett is professor of business administration at Harvard Business School. Samantha Ghoshal is Professor of Business Policy at INSEAD (in Europe).

What are they famous for?

Bartlett and Ghoshal were famous for stressing that competition was now taking place across global markets, and not just in national markets. This book was very much focused on identifying the critical competencies of the transnational. Effectively they tackled the imperatives and dilemmas of how to manage across borders, particularly within matrix structures.

How are they linked with other gurus?

Bartlett and Ghoshal have links with other writers who have studied global competition – including Hamel and Prahalad, Porter, Pascale and Yip. Their contribution has been very much about 'Think globally, but act locally' – suggesting that a global strategy still needs to be closely tailored to the local environment. Bartlett and Ghoshal describe the ways in which they see the Transnational corporation as being managed as an integrated network of strategic business units. This involves developing centres of excellence worldwide and also ensuring that learning is spread between these units.

What is their main work?

'Managing Across Borders', Harvard Business School Press, Boston Mass 1989 – which is a combination of a rigorous research project and a prescriptive discussion of how organisations should think and act to be more global.

What are their main concepts?

Global strategy.

Ease of reading – medium.

G Bennett-Stewart

Who is G Bennett-Stewart?

G Bennett-Stewart is a US-based management consultant who coined the idea of 'EVA'.

What is he famous for?

He is famous for coining the expression of EVA; or Economic Value Added. Put simply, 'economic value added' is the present value of future cash flows which is in excess of that required to service the cost of capital.

EVA has won over a large number of major corporations, particularly in the US as being a way to financially evaluate both new and existing business strategies. It can also be used to evaluate possible areas for corporate disposal and closure. Equally it both can and must be used to evaluate any new acquisition or alliance.

EVA is a measure which is based on cash flow rather than on conventional accounting profit measurement. Cash flows are that much closer to the economic worth of a business than accounting profit (accounting profit being distorted by many non-cash adjustments (like depreciation). A further benefit of the EVA approach is that it does take into account longer-term cash flows whereas accounting profit is merely shorter term. Also, using EVA it is possible to trade off long and short cash flows thereby avoiding short-termism in the economic valuation of strategic decisions.

EVA can thus be used as an additional evaluation tool which will complement more qualitative, strategic analysis in:

- Corporate strategy.
- Acquisitions and mergers.
- Alliances.
- Business strategy.
- Strategic investment decisions.
- Targeting the value of strategic change.
- More effective cost management.

What are his main links to other gurus?

He is closely linked to McTaggart et al, Reimann and Rappaport.

What is his main work?

'The Quest for Value', HarperCollins, New York, 1991 – This is a very clear account of how to plan for shareholder value creation and how to evaluate and manage the cost of capital.

What are his main concepts?

Economic value added (or EVA).

Ease of reading – more difficult.

Blackadder

Who was Blackadder?

Blackadder was a famous TV series starring Rowan Atkinson as a jovial character set in the past.

What was he famous for?

Blackadder was famous for his 'cunning plans'. Indeed, an alternative definition of strategy is 'strategy is the cunning plan'.

As an example of a 'cunning plan' in the Blackadder millennium video, Blackadder and Baldrick invent a time machine. Before they are ready to set off one of them falls on the controls, sending them back into the past.

Unfortunately they cannot remember the original time settings, and although they are enjoying themselves disrupting the past, eventually want to get back to the present. In frustration, Blackadder says to Baldrick:

"So I am condemned to spend the rest of my life in a small room with two toilets, with the stupidest man on earth."

To which Baldrick replies:

"Don't worry, because I think I have a cunning plan."

To which Blackadder says,

"I am sceptical, what is your 'cunning plan'?"

Baldrick outlines his plan:

"You know how when people drown, there life flashes back in front of their eyes. If you were to stick your head in a bucket of water, just until the moment you were about to die, then you would remember the settings, and we could all go home."

"Cunning plan", said Blackadder, "with one or two minor improvements…."

And in the next scene we see Blackadder putting Baldrick's head down the toilet. Not content with Baldrick's cunning plan, Blackadder has made a stunning plan.

A cunning plan thus typically:

- starts off with the objective – 'what do I really, really want?' – in this case, remembering the settings.

- brings together some possible solutions in a novel combination – for looking at how you might remember something you have forgotten.

- at least one of these solutions is relatively surprising and not obvious – it certainly is not an obvious solution.

- but the total package (the whole cunning plan) is relatively simple at bottom.

- and also, preferably, relatively hard to imitate.

In summary, Blackadder's definition of strategy, the cunning plan, is a useful and light antidote to some of the heavier guru books on strategy.

What are his main concepts?

The cunning plan.

Boston Consulting Group

Who is the Boston Consulting Group?

The Boston Consulting Group (or BCG) is a major strategy consulting firm which thrived originally in the 1960s and has become an international organisation working with innumerable major companies worldwide.

What is BCG famous for?

BCG is famous for the market growth/market share matrix (see Figure 8). On the vertical axis we see relative market growth. On the horizontal axis we see relative market share.

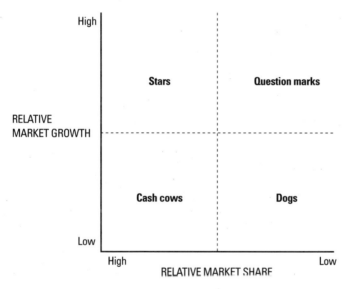

FIGURE 8: THE BCG MATRIX

The grid is split up into four main quadrants:

- North west: 'stars' – growth businesses.
- South west: 'cash cows' – harvest businesses.
- North east: ' question marks – emerging businesses.
- South east: 'dogs' – businesses which are candidates for divestment.

Typically over its lifetime a business might start off as a Question Mark, then become a Star, and then in maturity become a Cash Cow, fading eventually into a Dog. The matrix thus helps not only with portfolio analysis but also with the life cycle analysis of company products.

The BCG matrix (or grid) is a crude way of evaluating portfolio strategic business units. However, it suffers from a number of dangerous disadvantages as follows:

- 'Relative market growth' is only one dimension of attractiveness, ignoring the PEST factors and Porter's five forces.

- 'Relative market share' is only one variable of competitive positioning (you need to consider also: brand, product quality, service, responsiveness, unit costs etc).

- The definition of 'relative market share' can be fudged depending on market definition (e.g. niche local or global).

- The presumption that you should divest of Dogs is potentially dangerous and inappropriate: actually, under the BCG definition, most businesses are actually dogs.

- The matrix can easily be taken to imply that the positionings are givens and final – they are not, but are merely starting points for thinking imaginatively about the strategic business unit.

What are their main concepts?

- Stars, cash cows, dogs and question-mark businesses;
- portfolio analysis.

Reading verdict – Don't use it!

Cliff Bowman

Who is Cliff Bowman?

Cliff Bowman is Professor of Strategic Management at Cranfield School of Management in the UK.

What is he famous for?

Cliff Bowman is mainly famous for his highlighting the need to work out the quotient of:

$$\frac{\text{Perceived Use Value}}{\text{Relative Price}}$$

Whilst some would think this a relatively obvious thing to work out or position on a two-by-two-grid (see Figure 9) it would appear (from practical application, and from research), this is typically not the case.

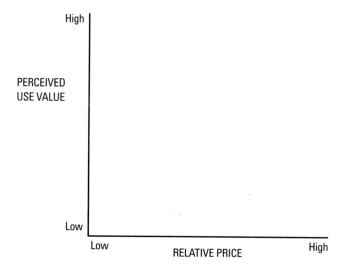

FIGURE 9: PERCEIVED USE VALUE/RELATIVE PRICE

In the grid in Figure 9 the best quadrant to be positioned in is where there is a very high perceived use value, and low relative price (top left). This leads to more sustainable growth and a strong competitive position. The weakest position is to have a low perceived use value and a high relative price – the symptom of a company that has become complacent and lost its way.

More difficult again is where you have a high perceived use value but the relative price is very high, too. So, for example, the author is organising a business trip to Microsoft in Seattle. He has only three options to fly direct with British Airways: economy (£1,150), British Airways World Traveller Plus – slightly better than economy (£1,550) and business class (over £6,000!). Microsoft are incredulous about the £6,000, and require much persuasion to pay World Traveller Plus. And who are Microsoft? One of the most successful companies in the world (as at 2002)!

Perhaps British Airways has problems, here?

Bowman has also worked excessively on the tacit competencies which often play a major role in determining competitive advantage. For instance, in one of his cases it turned out that the main ingredient in one Company's competitive edge was the particularly clever way in which the sales force got client buy-in.

To identify these tacit competencies is often very hard from the inside of an organisation, as they are taken for granted. It often needs some customer input, some independent observations of key value – creating activities vis a vis customers, and outside facilitation.

Whilst being thoroughly researched, Cliff Bowman's work is a refreshing antidote to strategy theories which seem remote and practical.

What other gurus does he link to?

Bowman's work on tacit competencies is closely linked with Hamel and Prahadad 1994. It also moves well beyond Porter's generic strategies. His practical emphasis is parallel to that of the author himself (as 'alternative guru').

Also, his comparison of perceived use value (or PUV) against price helps us with Porter's assertion (see later section on Michael Porter) that you can't pursue a differentiation and cost leadership simultaneously to be successful. For Bowman, the essence of competitive strategy was to be found in providing greater perceived value (relative to price) – relative to your competitors.

What are his main works?

'The Essence of Competitive Strategy', Prentice Hall, 1995.

What are his main concepts?

- Perceived use value (PUV); and
- the PUV/relative price grid.

Ease of reading – relatively easy.

Braybrooke and Lindblom

Who are Braybrooke and Lindblom?

Braybrooke and Lindblom were process-school theorists who highlighted the lack of structure (and equally logic) in the strategic decision-making process in most organisations.

What were they really famous for?

Their book characterised strategic decision-making in organisations as being fundamentally uncertain and chaotic, and as being naturally hostile to the idea of formal strategic planning.

The merits of their work are that it provides a healthy check on naïve attempts to install a strategic planning process which does not reflect – and take into account of the behavioural realities. Whilst highly analytical systems like Ansoff's (1965) focus on environmental scanning, SWOT analysis, gap analysis etc., and do provide some structure to strategic thought, they do not always map on easily to the existing management process. To combat the difficulties of muddling through one might:

- deploy a number of analytical, strategic analysis techniques, but without expecting them to, in themselves, deliver strategic insights and change without managing organisational politics on parallel.

- have an off-site.

- reflect on team-roles beforehand.

- use a facilitator.

What are their links with the other gurus?

Braybrooke and Lindblom pre-dated Quinn's work (1980) on 'logical incrementalism' – which painted a slightly more rational account of strategic decision-making, and also of Mintzberg's emergent strategy, which again emphasised the fluidity of the strategy process. Their ideas also link in with the need for organisational learning to deliver real strategic thinking (Argyris 1991, Senge 1990).

What are their main works?

Braybrooke D and Lindblom C E. 'A Strategy of Decision', New York, Free Press, 1963 – how organisations muddle through in the strategic – decision-making process.

What are their main concepts?

Muddling through.

Ease of reading – difficult.

Campbell A and Goold (major gurus – despite being in the UK)

Who are Campbell and Goold?

Campbell and Goold were both ex strategy consultants who moved over into strategy academia in the early 1980s. They are two of the rare number of UK strategy thinkers to penetrate the Harvard Business Review. They are perhaps more closely associated with the deliberate school of strategy, with their analytical concerns, but this does not mean that they are unaware of the process perspective throughout their thinking.

What are they famous for?

Campbell and Goold wrote both 'Strategies and Styles' (1987) and the 'meaty' text 'Corporate-Level Strategy' (1994). Their first book 'Strategies and Styles' distinguished between three types of corporate style, being:

- The strategic planning style: where the centre dominates not only the 'why?' of business strategies, but also its 'what?'.

- The strategic control style: here the corporate centre may set the ground rules (the 'why?') but the 'what' and the 'how' are mainly down to the strategic business units.

- The financial control style: in this style the centre is very focused indeed on delivering the financial numbers, and is 'hands-off' if these are delivered well, and 'hands-on' if they are not.

The main point in this typology is that the corporate parent needs to make choices in a) how it is going to interrelate with its strategic business units – choosing between the above styles and b) in also the areas as a centre it will add value or not add, to its portfolio (for example in the provision of central services).

The author used this typology over a decade ago with the Cookson Group, a conglomerate in materials processing (originally metals). There was a great debate over whether the group was a 'financial control' or a 'strategic control' company – there was (then) an obvious ambiguity over how the group was managing strategy. This debate was very helpful as very senior managers had previously been getting somewhat confused and frustrated at apparent contradictions in the centre's role/their roles.

Campbell and Goold obviously realised quite quickly that whilst their typology was insightful and useful it required refinement. Campbell and Goold then furthered this work by extensive empirical research on synergies – within Groups. Perhaps, not surprisingly, they discovered that the economic value of synergies is highly elusive. The main reasons for this appear to be:

- Managers' main (and natural) preoccupation is with harvesting the value of their own business limits, rather than in collaborating in the hoped-for delivery of value with other business units.

- Internal, political rivalry, which reduced cooperation in many companies.

- Structurally, it is difficult to manage synergies across organisational and cultural boundaries.

- Without recognising a rewarding managers explicitly for harvesting synergies, managers simply will not do it.

Besides their earlier ground-breaking work (along with Marcus Alexander), they also contributed to strategic thought with their thoroughly researched book on corporate parenting, 'Corporate Level Strategy' (1994). This looked at the conditions for corporate parents actually adding value to their business portfolios, through identifying opportunities, avoiding value-destruction, through influencing stand-alone businesses to do certain strategic things, and through synergies. One of their main concepts is that of 'parenting advantage' – very simply it asks what the corporate parent is really good at, rather than merely competitive advantage primarily.

One of their main findings was that synergy value is highly elusive, and is often not really worth trying to manage. This is due to their complexity and their lack of appeal, and to the common agendas of different stakeholders.

What are their links to other gurus?

Campbell and Goold have operationalised Ansoff's earlier account (1965) of corporate planning by looking at the *style* of corporate planning, as opposed to its *process* and *context*, linking this style too to both corporate culture and structure. They are also loosely linked with the Shareholder Value movement, focusing on the value of the corporate centre, although they fall short of an in-dept interest in quantification of economic value. As gurus, they have tried to position themselves as the ordinary Porter's of Competitive Strategy and with some success.

What are their main works?

1 'Strategies and Styles', Basil Blackwell, Oxford 1987 (Campbell and Goold): An important work suggesting that corporate Group's can manage corporate strategy in a variety of dissimilar ways – highlighting that you need to choose.

2 'Corporate Level Strategy', John Wiley, New York 1994 (Goold, Campbell and Alexander): a thorough treatment of how corporate strategy can create value.

What are their main concepts?

- Strategic planning;
- strategic control and financial control styles;
- parenting advantage/corporate value added;
- corporate synergy.

Ease of reading – medium.

Alfred Chandler (a major guru)

Who is Alfred Chandler? ·

Alfred Chandler was a very famous academic strategist who pre-dated Michael Porter, and who provided an early and rigorous account of the relationship between strategy and business structure. He is perhaps better known in the US than in Europe. He is more closely associated with the 'deliberate' or 'rationale' school of strategic management rather than the process school.

What is he famous for?

Chandler's seminal work 'Strategy and Structure' suggested that before business structure is defined, the business strategy itself must be clarified. His thoughts fed into McKinsey's development of the idea of 'Strategic Business Units'. A 'Strategic Business Unit' (or SBU) can be defined as:

'A set of similar customer needs, similar customer types, and similar ways of delivering value to those target customers.'

So, for example, SBU's at Manchester United might include:

- Media (broken down into terrestrial, Sky, own SkyChannel – MUKV, Internet, mobiles)
- Merchandising
- Corporate entertainment
- Catering
- The team itself

Typically many companies are organised around more arbitrary lines than the above, (especially in the much earlier period of the1960s) and often contain a mass of different business models. By extolling the virtues of 'think market first, organisation second', Chandler helps us to define organisational structure more effectively.

What are his main links with the other gurus?

Chandler's view of strategy is very much based on economic analysis, and paved the way for Ansoff (1965) and later on Porter (1980, 1985).

What are his main works?

'Strategy and Structure', Cambridge MA, MIT Press, 1962: How decentralised units facilitate strategic management.

What are his main concepts?

Strategy should precede structure in business design.

Ease of reading – medium.

A De Geus

Who is De Geus?

De Geus was a former senior strategic planner at Shell who was instrumental in developing its scenario process, who moved into more academic work.

What is he famous for?

De Geus was notable for outlining and popularising the key principles of scenario planning:

- 'Scenarios' are story-lines of the future which give it a dynamic picture. These story-lines are merely possibilities – which are both internally consistent, and also have a good degree of plausibility.

- The purpose of scenario development is to give us insights about possible futures – and absolutely not to make forecasts.

- The future story-line can be developed by identifying the key environmental systems which will shape the future, for example, the political, the economic, the market, competition, customers and innovation.

- The shift from the present would to some future world occur by identifying possible *transitional* events – these give rise to either 'weak signals' Ansoff), or potentially strong symptoms.

What are his links with the other gurus?

De Geus is associated with systems thinking (Senge 1990), strategy as learning (Argyris 1991) and with environmental scanning (Ansoff 1965) and Wack 1985 (also of scenario development). This has been taken further in the world of IT strategy in the notion of 'disruptive technologies'.

What are his main works?

'Planning as Learning', Harvard Business Review, March-April pp70-74, 1988.

What are his main concepts?

Scenarios and discontinuities.

Ease of reading – relatively easy.

Eliyahu Goldratt

Who was Goldratt?

Goldratt was a writer whose novel 'The Goal' focused on decision-making by identifying the most limiting constraint at each stage of the decision-making process, resolving it, and moving on to the next one.

What is he famous for?

Goldratt's focus on constraints is helpful because it assists strategists to focus on blind-spots during implementation, rather than getting carried away by blue sky ideas.

What are his links with the other gurus?

Goldratt's work has linkages with other major themes in management:

- **force field analysis:** (see Lewin (1935), later on): which identifies and prioritises constraining forces.

- **critical path analysis (from project management):** which tells us to identify that series of activities which is the most limiting constraint.

- **operational research:** where linear programming attempts to optimise a solution to a problem where there is a limiting constraint.

Goldratt's practicality is a powerful antidote to the perhaps over-prescriptive and sometimes hyped works of writers like Kanter 1983, Peters 1982 and Pascale 1990.

What are his main works?

1   'The Goal' North River Press, Great Barrington Mass, 1985 – A novel based on eliminating the constraints, one by one (actually in a particular project).

2   'Theory of Constraints', North River Press, Great Barrington, Mass, 1990 – A more conventional management text explaining the basis for these colours.

What are his main concepts?

The concept of focusing on the limiting constraint.

Ease of reading – medium.

Robert Grant

Who is Robert Grant?

Robert Grant was a US strategy academic who challenged Porter's views on the basis for competitive advantage. He suggested that competitive advantage was more frequently to be discovered in access to distinctive or unique internal resources, rather than a choice between the different forms of generic strategies externally (see Porter 1985).

What was he famous for?

Grant was famous for suggesting that insights about competitive positioning were more likely to come from understanding a company's resource base rather than from its generic strategies. He particularly focused on the extent to which organisations had non-immitatable resources.

One example of unique resources was the company Video Arts, set up by John Cleese to exploit his talents as a spoof manager in management training videos. Of course, there is only one John Cleese, and these videos sold extremely well – and at a high margin. There was not, at the time, any real competition and fewer real substitutes.

In its heyday, Video Arts had a turnover of £2 million per year and a net profit of £1 million – a return in sales of a staggering fifty per cent – a very good return on non-immitatable resources.

What are their links with the other gurus?

Grant's work has close links to Hamel and Prahalad 1994 – in the form of 'core competencies'. In many ways Grant's 'resources' and Hamel and Prahalad's 'core competencies' overlap to a considerable extent. His concepts have also been taken further by Bowman (1995).

What is his main work?

'The Resource-Based Theory of Competitive Advantage', Californian Management Review pp114-135, 33, 3, 1991 – How acquiring a unique set of resources is the key to competitive advantage.

What are his main concepts?

- Imitability;
- resource-based competitive advantage.

Ease of reading – difficult.

Tony Grundy
(the alternative guru – the author)

Who is Tony Grundy?

The author is a former chartered Accountant, and an MBA and PhD who has researched strategic decision-making, strategic thinking, strategic behaviour and organisation strategy. He has spent much of his career as a management consultant, now in parallel with a senior lecturer role at Cranfield School of Management.

What has he contributed?

The author has made a number of contributions to strategic management, including for example:

- Into the links between strategic decision-making and shareholder value. (Grundy 1992, 1998b, 2002a).

- Into the role of creative and innovative thinking in strategic management (Grundy 1993, 1994, 2002b).

- Growth drivers – which determine the rate of market growth (Grundy 1994, 2002) – see Figure 10.

- The strategy implementation process (Grundy 1993, 2001).

- The behaviours associated with strategy (Grundy 1998).

- The management of strategic acquisitions (Grundy 1994, 2002).

- The (economic) value of strategic thinking (2002).

- Organisation/HR strategy (Grundy 2003).

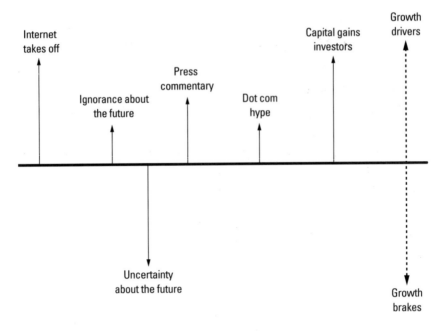

FIGURE 10: GROWTH DRIVERS

Linking strategic decision-making and shareholder value: Grundy (1992) looked at why strategic decisions can be hard to put an (economic) value on, and how to deal with the problems of interdependency, intangibles, and uncertainty. Most of these problems dissolved when a number of qualitative methodologies were used (like Mitroff's uncertainty-importance grid – see Mitroff).

Grundy (1998b, 2002a) expands these concepts into a more rounded account of the constellation of value-creating activities (the 'business value system') and in managing key value and cost drivers which is a more flexible concept. Grundy also suggested Porter's value chain (that conventional strategic analysis) is typically limited to defining the problem/opportunity within its current diagnosing definition, rather than challenging the art of the possible. In particular, he put forward the idea of a sixth competitive force, (to complement Michael Porter's five forces) – of the 'industry-mind-set'. The 'industry mind-set' is defined as 'the set of expectations, perceptions and assumptions currently prevalent in an industry'.

He also evolved a more refined version of Mintzberg's two forms of strategy into five. These comprise (see Figure 11):

- Deliberate strategy.
- Emergent strategy.
- Submergent strategy (escalating commitment to a wobbly strategy).
- Emergency strategy (disparate attempts to turn it around).
- Divergent strategy (sorting the mess out, afterwards).

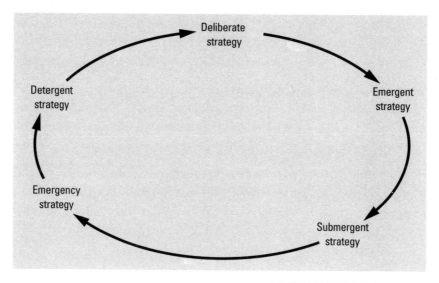

FIGURE 11: THE STRATEGY MIX

The 'strategy mix' is a helpful diagnostic tool which purports the current predominant form of strategy prevalent in an organisation.

The strategy implementation process

Unlike many authors (whose primary interest is in strategic analysis and choice) the author has developed an integrated process to help shape strategic implementation (Grundy 1992, 1994, 2001, 2002). Aspects of this process have been adopted formally within HSBC, Microsoft, Nokia, Royal Bank of Scotland, Standard Life and Tesco.

The author's research into strategic behaviour at BT (or how its managers interact to develop and discuss strategy) also highlighted that:

- Many internal disputes about strategy are due to implicit (and not so well revealed) personal agendas.

- To work well as a strategic team, a very large and complex number of organisational factors need to be aligned.

- Surprisingly the use of analytical techniques can (of itself) dissolve a large proportion of political and inter-personal difficulties.

On a more process-related topic, the author has developed a useful management process for dealing with strategic acquisitions (Grundy 2002). This process integrating strategic, and financial, and organisational perspectives.

The author's research into HR/organisational strategy suggests that this should be owned by line management, and not by HR. It also indicates that the analytical processes required for strategy implementation provide effective ways of dealing with less tangible HR/organisational strategy issues.

Finally, the author's research with Brown (Grundy and Brown 2002b), highlighted that strategic thinking (and more specifically, strategic thoughts) can generate considerable shareholder value. Unfortunately, managers tend not to define the economic value created by them, and this tends to undermine the strategic thinking capability in many organisations.

What are his links to other gurus?

The author borrows equally from both the 'design' and 'process' schools of strategy (Porter 1985) and Mintzberg (1994). He is also closely linked in with the literature on shareholder value management (McTaggart et al, etc). There are also close parallels with the emphasis on innovation from Hamel and Prahalad.

What are his main works?

1 'Corporate Strategy and Financial Decisions', (1992) – the role of strategic investments in strategy formulation.

2 'Implementing Strategic Change', (1992) – tools and processes for managing strategic change.

3 'Strategic Learning in Action', (1993) – using learning to drive strategic thinking.

4 'Breakthrough Strategies for Growth', (1994) – tools and cases for developing breakthrough strategies in Europe.

5 'Harnessing Strategic Behaviour', (1998a) – lessons from research at BT into the impact of management behaviour on strategy.

6 'Exploring Strategic Financial Management', (1998b) – the sister book to Johnson and Scholes 'Exploring Corporate Strategy' – linking strategic and financial analysis.

7 'Strategic Project Management', (2002a) – a unique guide to managing projects as mini-strategies.

8 'Acquisitions and Mergers', (2002b) – an exhaustive account of the strategic, financial and other implications of acquisitions.

9 'Be Your Own Strategy Consultant – Demystifying Strategic Thinking', (2002) – an updated and complete account of practical strategic thinking and of its contribution to shareholder value.

10 'Growth', (2002d) – a concise guide to managing growth.

11 'Shareholder value', (2002e) – an overview of content and process issues in managing for shareholder value.

12 'Value-Based HR strategy', Butterworth Heinnemann, (2003 forthcoming) – a complete toolkit for how to manage HR strategy – and for shareholder value.

What are his main concepts?

- The strategy mix;
- the industry mind-set;
- growth drivers;
- the business value system;
- valuing strategic thinking;
- strategic project management;
- breakthroughs;
- the strategic option grid.

Ease of reading – relatively easy.

Gary Hamel and S K Prahalad (major gurus)

Who are Hamel and Prahalad?

Hamel and Prahalad are eminent gurus of strategy. They are more closely associated with the deliberate school of strategy.

Gary Hamel is Professor of Strategic Management at London Business School. He has researched strategy development in a multinational context.

What are they famous for?

Hamel and Prahalad are famous for three main contributions:

- Core competencies.
- Competing in the future.
- Innovation in strategy.

Core competencies

A core competence is a cluster of skills which either enables us to compete, or gives us a distinctive way of competing. Unfortunately, it is not always easy to identify an organisation's core competencies from the inside, as these competencies are often taken for granted and of a tacit nature. It is often easier to assess these from the outside, particularly by examining customers' perspectives of the organisation.

For example, Ryan Air's core competencies are:

- Low cost mind-set.
- Low cost management and operational processes.

Offsetting these competencies are also Ryan Air's not-so-good competencies in:

- Media management.
- Handling customer complaints.
- Dealing with customers as individuals.

Core competencies will change over time and these changes need to be built into future organisational strategy.

Competing for the future

Hamel and Prahalad's book 'Competing for the Future' is an accessible, imaginative and a 'must-read' book. The authors do not see any industry as a 'given' but refreshingly, are willing to entertain a variety of possible futures, which can then be created. (They belong to the 'visionary school'.) Whilst many MBA's get over-focused on analysing what currently exists, – in industries and markets, rather than what *might* be there, – Hamel and Prahalad focus on stretching out mind-sets and on our powers of imagination. This line of thought is encapsulated within the author's own concept of 'Breakthrough Strategic Thinking', which regards strategy as a creative, imaginative – and analytical process. Companies that have delivered deliberate breakthrough strategies in the past ten years include:

- Dyson: carpet cleaning.
- Manchester United: merchandising and media.
- Tesco: diversification into non-food, higher value products.

Finally, Hamel and Prahalad underline the importance of innovation in strategy and of introducing more playfulness into strategic thinking sessions, thus de-emphasising planning bureaucracy.

What are the links with the other gurus?

Hamel and Prahalad have effectively picked up on Kenichi Ohmae's definition of competitive advantage and taken it into the future. They are also not entirely dissimilar to Pascale, Peters and Kanter, who are trying to challenge the existing organisational mind-set.

What are their main works?

1   'The Core Competence of the Corporation', Harvard Business Review, pp79-91, May-June 1990 – understanding the specific bases of competitive advantage.

2   'Strategic Intent', Harvard Business Review, pp63-76, May-June 1989 – strategic intent is more specific than mission, very similar to vision.

3   'Strategy as Stretch and Leverage', Harvard Business Review, 71, 2, pp75-84, March-April 1993 – looking at how strategy can stretch your view of the possible.

4   'Competing for the Future', Harvard Business School Press Boston, Mass 1994 – imagining and creating the future rules of the game.

What are their main concepts?

- Core competencies;
- strategic intent;
- breakthroughs;
- challenging mind-set;
- future thinking.

Ease of reading – relatively easy.

Charles Handy
(a major guru – and from the UK)

Who is Charles Handy?

Charles Handy is one of the very few, major UK gurus, for many years a professor at London Business School.

What is he famous for?

Charles Handy was to strategic management what Phil Collins was to pop music. (Phil Collins was part of the band Genesis who produced a number of off-the-wall albums in the 1970's which had a cult following, but never sold in vast volumes.)

Then he produced albums of wider and simpler appeal and became extremely successful. Charles Handy's original book on 'Organisations' was a well thought through, academic account of different organisational forms which underpinned strategy through structure. But it was not until much later that Handy became both popular and famous, with his more accessible book and also his book on 'The Empty Raincoat' – on the virtual organisation. Handy always likes to be at the leading edge of thinking, especially in the cultural and ethical issues associated with management.

What are his main links to other gurus?

Handy's work was parallel with Rosebeth Moss Kanter in the US, with her emphasis on empowerment and on new forms of careers for senior managers (see next guru).

What are his main works?

1   'Understanding Organisations', Penguin, 1976 – a systematic account of generic organisational structures and how they operate (still used on some MBA courses).

2   'The Empty Raincoat', Hutchinson, London, 1994 – a challenging account of the 'virtual organisation' where a core workforce is surrounded by outsourced (mainly home) workers.

What are his main concepts?

- The virtual organisation;
- organisational forms;
- governance.

Ease of reading – easy.

P Haspeslagh and D Jemison

Who are Haspeslagh and Jemison?

Phillipe Haspeslagh and David Jemison are two leading strategy academics who have studied the strategic aspects of acquisitions. Haspeslagh is Professor of Business Policy at INSEAD, and Jamison is Professor of Management at the University of Texas.

What are they famous for?

They are famous for providing the first comprehensive, theoretical and practical account of the strategic management of academics. They highlighted in particular:

- The need to conduct a thorough strategic analysis of the acquiring company's own position, capability and options *before* commencing the acquisition search process.

- That acquisitions fall into different categories, such as domain protection or extension, and that a variety of different integration strategies may be appropriate, depending upon the particular acquisition context – for example relative autonomy versus absorption.

- Acquisition appraisal needs to be conducted with reference to how the two separate value-chains of acquirer and the acquired inter-relate and potentially complement (or duplicate) one another.

- Integration is a crucial phase of the acquisition process – and one where there is considerable chance of economic value being destroyed.

Their book contains some very useful input to in-company checklists for due diligence – both at the acquisition appraisal and integration stages of the process.

What are their links with the other gurus

'Managing Acquisitions' is closely linked to Porter's classic book on 'Competitive Advantage'. The book is also helpful as a support text for those readers wishing to think through how acquisitions add shareholder value (Reimann, Rappaport etc) and also in understanding the role of the corporate centre (Campbell and Goold).

What are their main works?

'Managing Acquisitions', The Free Press Macmillan, 1991 – a complete guide to the strategic management of acquisitions.

What are their main concepts?

- A typology of acquisitions;
- the importance of acquisition integration.

Ease of reading – relatively easy.

Gerry Johnson and Kevin Scholes (UK gurus)

Who are Johnson and Scholes?

Johnson and Scholes are acclaimed strategists who produced the first complete European textbook account of strategic management from the late 1980s through to the present time. Their UK textbook position is akin to the kind of dominance that Manchester United achieved in the 1990s through to 2001 in the strategy textbook industry. They are neither 'deliberate' or 'process' based in their classic textbook, but certainly Gerry Johnson is largely a process school thinker in his other works. Gerry Johnson's career includes professorial positions at Cranfield and at Glasgow, and Scholes at Sheffield Business School which he was formerly head of.

What are they famous for?

'Exploring Corporate Strategy' gives a comprehensive overview of strategic management concepts, techniques and approaches, right through from the analysis, choice and to implementation phase.

The book also contains extensive case material (which is continually being updated). Indeed the book has become a business, and even a strategy in its own right.

From a management students' perspective, here are some hints:

- Don't try to read it in a weekend – plan to read it in sections, perhaps over 6-8 weeks.

- Go back and re-read parts – strategic management is somewhat chicken-and-egg. Whilst Johnson and Scholes do an admirable job in presenting it in a particularly logical order, there are many interdependencies between the concepts, so you will need to re-read and review parts you have already read, to get the big picture.

- Don't take it on holiday – my partner did take it on holiday when she was doing her MBA. It never got opened and threatened to break our baggage weight limit!

What are their main links with the other gurus?

There is much value in reading their casebook: which gives you an excellent experience of doing a top-class MBA.

What are their main works?

'Exploring Corporate Strategy', Prentice Hall, Hemel Hempstead, 1989: this classic MBA text deals with analysis, choice, and implementation as the key stages of strategic management. This very comprehensive book is accompanied by a wealth of up-to-date case studies.

What are their main concepts?

- Strategic fit;
- the paradigm;
- the strategy process.

Ease of reading – difficult (but only due to the volume of their work, so don't let this put you off). This book needs to be read over a period of weeks, chapter by chapter.

Rosebeth Moss Kanter (a major guru)

Who is Rosebeth Moss Kanter?

Rosebeth Moss Kanter is a US Sociologist and Harvard Business School Professor who has developed a theory of change management. She consults with major companies and is a fearless critic of traditional management thinking.

What is she famous for?

Kanter is famous for being an early guru of strategy implementation. She was a major exponent of empowerment and (rightly) highlighted the need to increase total power in the organisation (to actually implement a strategy) – as a positive sum game. (A 'positive sum game is one where all parties are better off – then they would otherwise be – after collaborating.) Her main books (see below) are long and contain a large quantity of semi-prescriptive case studies. But she may still be worthwhile reading in the original.

Her central ideas are:

- that major corporations need to be lean, and able to do more with less, and to be proactive in seeking change, rather than resisting it.

- the individuals in the organisation need to be empowered so that they can implement strategy, rather than have intrusive interventions from on high.

- the structure of individuals' careers is far more likely to be fluid – with more portable careers than previously.

What are her links with the other gurus?

Kanter is part of the management movement (which included Peters 1982 and Pascale 1990) who focused on the interrelationships between strategy and organisational change. (See also Welch 2001.)

What are her main works?

1   'The Change Masters: Corporate Entrepreneurs at Work', Schuster, New York, 1994.

2   'When Giants Learn to Dance', Simon and Schuster, New York, 1989.

What are her main concepts?

- Empowerment;
- contention;
- de-layering.

Ease of reading – relatively easy.

Kaplan and Norton (major gurus)

Who are Kaplan and Norton?

Kaplan is a Harvard Business School Professor whilst Norton is the co-founder of the IT strategy consultants, Nolan and Norton. Their work is more in keeping with the 'deliberate strategy' school, approaching it from an operational and financial perspective.

What are they famous for?

Kaplan and Norton are famous for developing the 'Balanced Score-Card' – as a means of:

a) not over-focusing on financial measures of performance; and

b) tracking the effective implementation of a strategy.

Their four key areas of control/measures are:

- Customer satisfaction.
- Operational efficiency.
- Employee morale.
- Financial performance.

The main idea of the balanced score-card is that one needs to measure and manage all of these indicators – and in balance, rather than primarily financial performance.

The original balanced score-card covers certain aspects of strategic control (customer satisfaction) well but not others, such as:

- relative strength vis a vis competitors
- innovation
- capability development

It also tends to over-emphasise short-term financial measurement over and above the generation of longer-term shareholder (or economic) value. But its biggest limitation is probably that it is very difficult to implement in most organisations – certainly without a lot of tailoring simplification and refinement. The author's own experience, for example, of helping implement a tailored, balanced score-card process within a division of HSBC is that:

- You need to identify your own, high-level, balanced score-card headings – relevant to your industry, organisation, and strategic agendas (a maximum of five).

- These headings need to be broken down into more specific, micro measures (perhaps three to five).

- The top team should not focus on all measures equally and simultaneously, but should focus each quarter in the year on a smaller number of areas where there is a performance gap.

What are their links to other gurus?

There are some links between the balanced score-card approach and the shareholder value/economic value-added (or EVA) literature, including Rappaport 1986, Reimann 1990 and McTaggart et al 1994 – as the non-financial aspects of the balanced score-card are in effect the indirect value drivers of the business.

What are their main works?

'The Balanced Score-Card – Measures that Drive Performance' (Kaplan RS & Norton DP), Harvard Business Review, pp71-90, January-February 1992.

What are their main concepts?

The Balanced Score-Card (and also Activity-Based-Costing: Kaplan).

Ease of reading – medium.

Kurt Lewin
(a major guru – albeit a long time ago)

Who was Kurt Lewin?

Kurt Lewin was a famous organisational theorist who devised a pictorial way of representing organisational change in the 1930s, which is still used today.

What was he famous for?

Lewin's 'force field' analysis splits out between:

- **the 'enablers':** the things that make change easier, from
- **the constraining forces:** the things that make change more difficult.

'Enablers' and 'constraints' might include for example: leadership, culture, resources, heyday, context, project management and existing workload/overload. An example of force field analysis is to be found in Chapter 4 on the Champney's Case.

Force field analysis creeps into MBA courses often in modules on strategic change. It is also taught on HR courses and is used by a minority of HR consultants/facilitators to examine implementation difficulty. Grundy and Brown ('Strategic Project Management', Thomson Learning, 2002) have attempted to popularise its use again.

What are his main links with other gurus?

Lewin's work is an important forerunner of the change school of the 1980s (Kanter, Peters and Waterman, Pascale). This technique has extended the use of force field analysis (see Grundy – 'Be Your Own Strategy Consultant' 2002) into many other domains of strategy.

What are his key concepts?

- Force field analysis;
- organisational resistances.

Ease of reading – medium.

P Lorange and J Roos

Who are Lorange and Roos?

Lorange and Roos are to strategic alliances what Haspeslagh and Jemison are to acquisitions. They are leading business school academics (Lorange at the Norwegian School of Management and Roos at Wharton in the US).

What are they famous for?

Lorange and Roos produced the first really classical account of how alliances need to be managed, and covered the international perspective. They distinguish between a variety of forms of alliance ranging from loose, collaboration arrangements with suppliers or distribution channels through to fully autonomous, separate joint ventures where the various partners take equity stakes in the business.

Lorange and Roos take essentially a *competitive perspective* on Alliances. They emphasise that the longer-term nature and success of a strategic alliance (where parties have a clear, longer-term stake in the alliance – of both money and usually management, too) is contingent on the relative bargaining power of the various partners. An alternative perspective is the collaborative – when an alliance is a 'positive sum' game between partners (i.e. where they are better off when they collaborate closely, so that they will tend to do just that).

What are their links with other gurus?

Lorange and Roos' book stands in relative isolation from the other gurus, although there is a need certainly, to tell scenario stories about their likely future evolution.

What is their main work?

'Strategic Alliances', Blackwell, Cambridge, Mass, 1992 – a complete account of the reliance, the dynamics and pitfalls of strategic alliances.

What are their main concepts?

Alliances as vehicles for competition.

Ease of reading – relatively easy.

McTaggart, Kontes and Mankins

Who are these gurus?

McTaggart, Kontes and Mankins were on the top staff at Marakon Associates, a value-based management consultancy. Marakon has been active in working at numerous companies including Alcan, Barclays Bank, BP, Cadbury Schweppes, ICI Paints, the Prudential and many others.

What are they famous for?

McTaggart et al have provided a very practical and relatively easy to read account of what 'Managing for (shareholder) Value' means – in terms of content, process and culture.

Managing for shareholder value is considered by them to be The Governing Objective of Corporates. They emphasise the need for a detailed assessment of potential for value creation through strategic decisions (via the value and cost drivers). They emphasise the importance of external, environmental value drivers much more than many other writers).

Their treatment of management process is particularly useful – including strategic planning budgeting, resource allocation, performance management, and top management corporation.

What are their main links with the other gurus?

Their work is closely linked with other shareholder value theorists like Rappaport 1996, Bennett Stewart 1991, Grundy 1998b, 2002e and Reinmann 1990.

Of these writers (along with Grundy) they also share links with Porter's economic models of strategic environments (five forces, value chain).

What is their main work?

'The Value Imperative' (McTaggart JM, Kontes PW and Mankins MC), The Free Press, Macmillan, 1994 – contains an accessible and informative guide to the strategic, financial and organisational implications of managing shareholder value.

What are their main concepts?

Value-based strategic management.

Ease of reading – relatively easy (given the subject matter).

Henry Mintzberg (a major guru)

Who is Henry Mintzberg?

Henry Mintzberg is a Canadian professor of strategic management at McGill University. He also holds a chair at INSEAD. He has, over several decades, been a leading figure in the strategy world. More of an academic than a prescriptive writer/consultant, his philosophy is based on how managers *actually create and implement* strategy, rather than how they *supposedly should do it.*

What is he famous for?

Mintzberg has also been a major contributor to the debate on the links between strategy and organisational structure. His 'organisational forms' predated Henry's later work on organisational structure and are a helpful way of understanding why different companies have vastly different structures and cultures.

Mintzberg's first major input came from studying managers at an everyday level. He found that whilst the theory was that managers should be reflective thinkers, the reality was that they were frenetic doers, lost in the momentum of management actions.

Mintzberg also looked at organisational structures, distinguishing:

- the 'strategic apex' – top executives.
- the 'technostructure' – the advisory stuff.
- the 'operating case' – the main doers.
- the 'middle line' – the supervisory force.
- the 'support staff' – R&D, HR etc.

This helped him to understand how organisational structures change over time to respond to market and company life cycles, and to thus adjust to strategic change. His book 'Structures in Fives' is perhaps a more comprehensive account of organisational structures than Handy's.

Most famous for his characterisation of strategy as messy and haphazard (sometimes however, falling into a coherent pattern of one form or another – or an 'emergent strategy'), he acted as a healthy counterbalance to the prescriptive theorists (like Ansoff and Porter).

Figure 12 gives an illustration of how the forms of strategy may operate: Deliberate strategies can be realised or unrealised, whilst emergent strategies simply materialise through action.

His weighty book 'The Rise and Fall of Strategies of Learning' (1994) argues that conventional planning processes are inappropriate to the more fluid decision-making process characteristic of most organisations.

Mintzberg (et al) also wrote one of the most enlightening books on strategy of recent times called 'Strategy Safari'. This likened the various schools of strategy (deliberate, process, visionary etc.) to the different kinds of animals which one would literally see – if one were, as it were, on safari. This is well worth a read, and will not put you to sleep!

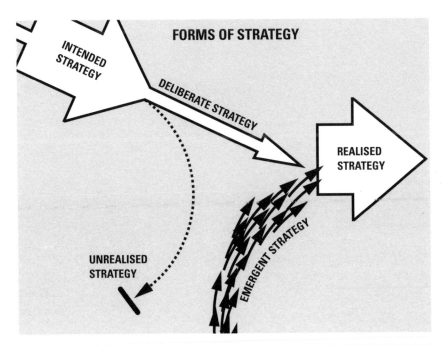

FIGURE 12: DELIBERATE AND EMERGENT STRATEGY

What are his links to the other gurus?

Mintzberg is part of the 'process' or 'incremental' school of strategic management alongside Braybrooke and Lindblom, and also Quinn.

What are his main works?

1   'The Nature of Managerial Work', Harper and Row, New York, 1973.

2   'The Structuring of Organisations', Prentice Hall, Englewood Cliffs, 1979 – an insightful analysis of organisational forms – and they relate to strategy.

3   'Structures in Fives: Designing Effective Organizations', Prentice Hall, New Jersey, 1983.

4   'The Rise and Fall of Strategic Planning', Prentice Hall, Hemel Hempstead, 1994 – a more than comprehensive, but slightly one-sided critique of conventional strategic planning.

5   'Strategy Safari' (Mintzberg H, Ahlstrand B and Lampel J), The Free Press, New York, 1998 – a humorous account by Mintzberg (and co-authors) of the diverse schools of strategic management.

What are his main concepts?

- Deliberate and emergent strategy;
- the design and process schools of strategy;
- organisational forms.

EASE OF READING

Strategy Safari – easy, essential reading.

The Rise and Fall of Strategic Planning – medium.

The Structuring of Organisations and Structures in Fives – more difficult.

Ian Mitroff

Who is Ian Mitroff?

Ian Mitroff is a Californian-based strategy guru with a direct, challenging style and who provided us with a framework for surfacing strategic assumptions. Mitroff is Professor of Business Policy at the University of Southern California.

What is he famous for?

Mitroff is famous for his contribution to helping uncover managers' mental maps of their strategy. He recognised that strategies often fail because of their dependency on taken-for-granted assumptions – which subsequently turn out not to be met. This called for an explicit process of mapping these assumptions, called the 'uncertainty-importance grid'.

The uncertainty-importance grid is illustrated in Figure 13. In its original form, the uncertainty grid appears somewhat abstract, so I have refined this by using four, generic descriptions for each quadrant. These include:

- very important and very uncertain: the 'danger zone'.
- very important and low uncertainty: 'the complacency zone'.
- low importance and very uncertain: 'the early warning zone'.
- low importance and low uncertainty: 'the trivial zone'.

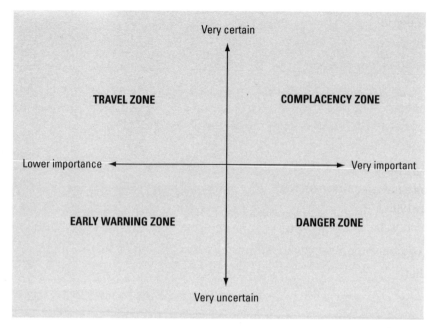

FIGURE 13: UNCERTAINTY-IMPORTANCE GRID

Mitroff's uncertainty-importance grid is an essential technique for scenario development. Typically a number of assumptions in the Danger Zone can be used to draw out a story-line for a future which is significantly different from the present. The uncertainty-importance grid can be used for:

- Acquisitions.
- Alliances.
- Restructuring.
- Managing strategic projects.
- Market entry.
- New product launch.

For example it has been used to track BMW's strategic decision to acquire Rover Group in 1994. (See Grundy's 'Breakthrough Strategic Thinking', Pitman, 1984 and 'Be Your Own Strategy Consultant', Thomson Learning, 2002.)

The grid suggested some major downsides to this decision including:

- Rover's high unit costs.
- The likelihood of major investment in Rover.
- The possibility of culture clash.
- Life cycles: Rover's four-wheel drive models maturing (the 'Discovery' range').

As a result of these uncertainties actually crystallising, Rover lost £900 million on a turnover of around £4,000 million in its last year of ownership by BMW in 1999, this being a salutary warning to those overlooking this essential technique.

When using the uncertainty-importance grid it is important to make sure that:

- The assumptions are spelt out in full – remember to ask the question: 'what is the big thing which we have forgotten?'
- The assumptions need to be set out quite explicitly – and with pre-determined parameters.
- Sometimes a highly critical assumption needs to be broken down into its sub-assumptions.

What are his links with the other gurus?

Mitroff straddles the divide between the deliberate strategy school and the process-school. The uncertainty-importance grid helps the formation of both deliberate and emergent strategies. Not only this, but it also reflects a concern for the strategic management process – which is often *implicit* rather than explicit.

Mitroff's questioning of the assumption-set of managers also links to Hamel and Prahalad's (1994) emphasis on re-examining 'mind-sets', and also to the author's own work on Porter's sixth (missing) competitive force – the industry mind-set. (Note Grundy/Mitroff also make explicit use of systems thinking (linking him to Senge 1990.)

What is his main work?

'The Unbounded Mind'(Mitroff II and Linstrom HA), Oxford University Press, 1993: on how imaginative thinking is essential in strategy, and how assumptions need to be continually surfaced and examined (using the uncertainty-importance grid).

What are his main concepts

- Sustaining strategic assumptions;
- challenging mind-sets;
- the uncertainty-importance grid.

Ease of reading – medium to difficult.

Kenichi Ohmae

Who is Kenichi Ohmae?

Kenichi Ohmae was one-time Head of Strategy Consulting, McKinsey Japan. Ohmae's concise book 'The Mind of the Strategist' is a classic introductory book which is very accessible. This accessibility has assumed its very ready availability on book shelves for twenty years.

What is he famous for?

Ohmae was probably the first major thinker to define 'competitive advantage' and to do so just ahead of Michael Porter. He defined it as being:

> 'Either delivering superior value to your target customers relative to your competitors, or, delivering equivalent customer value to your target customers relative to your competitors at least cost.'

This is embodied in his 'Three Cs' model (see Figure 14), for actually thinking through the idea of competitive position. To actually use this in practice we would also need to have previously researched:

- Customer bench-marking of the company (in terms of perceived and real value-added) – vis a vis its customers.

- A more detailed appraisal of the strengths and weaknesses (including its cost base), vis a vis its competitors.

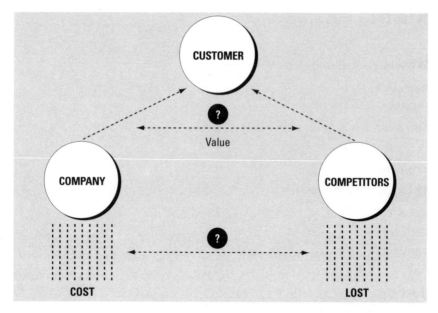

FIGURE 14: KENICHI OHMAE'S THREE 'C'S

What are his main links to other gurus?

Ohmae is linked closely with Michael Porter (1985), who created his generic strategies to help give some rules of thumb on the choice of a competitive strategy. He is also linked with Hamel and Prahalad (1994), who in 'Competing for the Future' essentially applied Ohmae's three cornered model within the context of the future, rather than merely of the present.

What are his main works?

'The Mind of the Strategist', New York, McGraw-Hill, 1982 – this is still in print and is one of the best and simplest introductions to strategic management.

What are his key concepts?

- Competitive advantage;
- competitive bench-marking;
- degrees of strategic freedom.

Ease of reading – easy.

R T Pascale (a major guru)

Who is Pascale?

Pascale was a leading business consultant and member of Stanford University's business school. He contributed to the Seven 'S' model of organisational success, popularised by Peters and Waterman in 1982.

What was he famous for?

Pascale was famous for his stress on contention and challenge in strategic management. Much of conventional strategic management focuses on logical analysis and thus on achieving consensus, whereas Pascale suggests that some degree of contention is actually fruitful.

How does his work link to the other gurus?

Pascal's work links closely with Kanter and Peters, who all share the agenda of challenging the organisation to think differently about key strategic issues.

What is his major work?

'Managing on the Edge' highlights this need for challenge in the ongoing processes of strategic diversion making and strategic change particularly through challenging paradigms. To do this he proposed that it was often essential to provoke debate, contention and conflict, which would then lead to strategic renewal. He also draws from studies of the ecology of natural organisms to help understand organisations as complex systems.

But perhaps his initial claim to fame was his work on 'The Art of Japanese Management' (Pascale and Athos 1981), which explained (using the seven 'S' model) how Japanese organisations were often superior. He contended that they were often better at managing the 'softer factors', particularly the 'shared values' (or superordinate gurus') than their western counterparts.

What are his major links to other gurus?

Pascale's major links are with Peters (and Waterman 1982), and of course with Senge 1990 (on systems thinking).

What are his main works?

1   'The Art of Japanese Management' (with Athos A Simon and Schuster), New York 1981) is a comparative study of organisational factors for strategic success between Japan and the US.

2   'Managing on the Edge?', Simon and Schuster, New York, 1990 – suggests that existing paradigms need to be challenged – through debate, contention and possibly conflict.

What are his key concepts?

- Challenging mind-sets;
- contention.

Ease of reading – relatively easy.

Tom Peters (a major guru)

Who is Tom Peters?

Tom Peters is a larger than life purveyor of challenging management ideas which have made more complacent top managers sit up and think – and for two decades. He is best known for his earliest book 'In Search of Excellence' (co-written with Robert Waterman).

What is he famous for?

'In Search of Excellence' was a piece of management research seeking to distil the lessons from a number of (then) high performing US companies. Peters and Waterman distilled from their research an organisational framework called the seven 's' model. 'In Search of Excellence' sold at least a million copies worldwide.

The seven 'S' model included:

- Strategy
- Structure
- Staff
- Skills
- Style
- Systems
- Shared values

The seven S's are indeed a useful checklist for making sure that in a particular organisational issue one has covered all the main angles. Separately, it is often useful to map the various interdependencies between the individual components of the seven S's, for example:

- Between strategy and structure.
- Between structure and style.
- Between style and share values etc.

Effectively this earlier model was based on the need for organisational align-ment (following a 'deliberate' strategy school model). Unfortunately, many of Peters and Waterman's earlier success stories actually went into decline (for example, IBM), causing him to revisit and even reverse earlier thinking. Peters and Waterman were caught out here by changing industry compe-tition, by complacency within the highly successful companies, and by sample, corporate life cycle effects.

Tom Peters went on (in 'Thriving On Chaos') to stress the antithesis to this alignment thinking by underlining the need for challenge, some disrup-tion and also for breaking the corporate mind-set, especially in more mature organisations.

Peters used the success of this later book to build a platform for world-wide Peter's workshops to spread the 'Thriving On Chaos' doctrine. Peters targeted corporate soft spots like internal mistrust and even the role of the HR departments whose control-led mind-set often *reduced* companies' competitive advantage, rather than added to it.

What is his main links to other gurus?

Peters is very much a part of the organisation redesign school which includes Pascale and Kanter. His challenge to existing mind-sets also echoes the work of Hamel and Prahalad, Mitroff and also of the author of this book. His earlier alignment model is very much along the lines of systems thinking and the learning organisation (Senge).

What are his main works?

1   'In Search of Excellence', Harper and Row, New York 1982 – this examines the conditions for success from the experience of major and leading companies during the 1970s.

2   'Thriving On Chaos', Alfred A Knopf, New York 1988 – Peters goes on to suggest that disruption to the status quo can actually be helpful, and provide the catalyst for change.

What are his main concepts?

- The seven 'S's;
- contention;
- thriving on chaos;
- downsizing;
- delayering.

Ease of reading – would be relatively easy if Peters wrote a little more succinctly. Otherwise medium to difficult.

Nigel Piercy

Who is Nigel Piercy?

Nigel Piercy was Professor of Marketing at Cardiff University. He is now a Professor of Marketing at Cranfield School of Management.

What is he famous for?

Nigel Piercy is famous for stakeholder analysis. His stakeholder analysis grid is shown in Figure 15, separating out attitude (for, neutral, against) from influence (high, medium, low). The grid is used mostly to map internal stakeholders, especially on a specific strategic decision. An example of a stakeholder analysis picture is contained in Chapter 4, Figure 24.

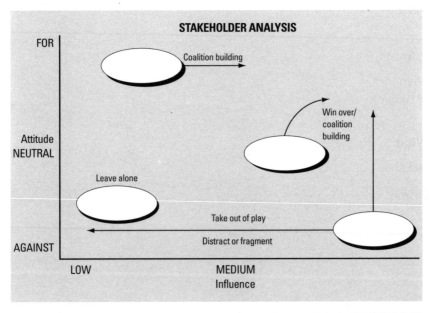

FIGURE 15: STAKEHOLDER ANALYSIS GRID

A 'stakeholder' can be defined as anyone inside or outside of the business who is either a decision-maker, adviser, implementer or victim of a strategy and of how it will be implemented.

The grid can be used:

- to analyse stakeholder positions (and their underlying agendas).
- to anticipate changes in who they are, or in their position.
- to devise cunning influencing plans.
- to reduce and dissolve organisational politics.

The grid has been developed in the author's own writings and is in everyday use at: CGNU, HSBC, Microsoft, Royal Bank of Scotland, Standard Life and Tesco.

How does he relate to other gurus?

Piercy's technique actually enables us to manage contention within more political organisations – without having overly destructive effects (Pascale 1990). It is also a most useful sister tool to Lewin's force field analysis (1935).

What is his main work?

'Diagnosing and Solving Problems of Strategy Implementation', Journal of General Management, pp19-38, Henley Vol 15, No 1, 1989.

What is his main concept?

Stakeholder analysis.

Ease of reading – medium.

Michael E Porter (a major guru)

Who is Michael Porter?

Michael Porter is Professor of Business Administration at Harvard Business School, and has also consulted with major corporations extensively. In 1983 he was appointed to the President's commission on industrial competitiveness. Michael Porter is a prolific author, best known for his two seminal works:

'Competitive Strategy' and 'Competitive Advantage'.

What is he famous for?

Porter is famous for a number of major innovations in strategy, particularly:

- Porter's five competitive forces.
- The value chain.
- the generic strategies: differentiation and cost leadership, focus.
- A critique of Internet strategies.

'Competitive Strategy' (1980) contains not just Porter's five competitive forces but also a comprehensive account of the evolution of markets throughout their life cycles.

Porter's five competitive forces address the question of 'why are some markets more attractive (in terms of long-term profitability) than others?' The answer is that they are more attractive than others because of structural reasons. This is down to (according to Porter), five key forces, namely:

- The bargaining power of the buyers.
- Entry barriers.
- Competitive rivalry.
- Substitutes.
- The bargaining power of the buyers.

Porter advises that each force should be appraised in terms of its relative attractiveness (high, medium or low). Porters five forces can give you a number of outputs:

- A better prioritisation of markets by their inherent attractiveness.
- A list of the critical success factors in the market, i.e. what things has *any* player got to get right/avoid getting wrong strategically to succeed.
- Providing insights for the criteria for judging yourself against competitors.

Ideas for changing the rules of the game (e.g. by reducing rivalry by acquisitions, shortening the value chain by going direct etc to the end-market) of value-creating activities.

THE VALUE CHAIN

Porter's value chain splits company operations into a number of generic components, namely:

- In-bound logistics.
- Manufacturing.
- Servicing.
- Sales and marketing.
- Administration.
- Out-bound logistics.

Essentially Porter's value chain is an (economists) 'input-output' model of how value is created in a business. It draws our attention to the internal choices which a company makes in determining how it is going to compete. The model can also be applied to an industry level, to look in particular at different ways of distributing products or services.

In its modern form it has been called 'the business model' – to indicate that it is specific to a particular business – Porter's headings above (like in-bound logistics) are not terribly helpful. Also it has been subsumed into the 'Business Value System' (Grundy 1998b) where not only is it drawn to be specific to a business, but instead of it being drawn as a linear, input-output analysis, it is depicted as more of a 'system' (Senge 1990). (See Figure 16) In more recent years his value chain has probably waned in popularity on business school courses. Not only is it perhaps one of the least exciting strategy tools to teach, but it does not often tell you an awful lot without a good deal of tailoring effort – to a specific industry context.

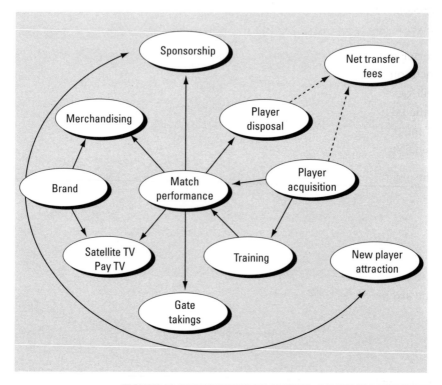

FIGURE 16: BUSINESS VALUE SYSTEM – FOOTBALL INDUSTRY

Porter's generic strategies comprises of: **differentiation, cost leadership,** and **focus**.

A '**differentiation**' strategy is one where you set out to add more value to your target customers (perceived and real) than your competitors do. This incremental value is manifest in either higher prices or discounts avoided, or both. A '**cost leadership**' strategy is one where you achieve parity of value with your competitors, but at a lower cost. Both generic strategies lead to above-average profitability.

A 'focus' strategy is where you have narrowed your competitive strategy to concentrate only on your target customers and their specific needs, and potentially also your product range. This aims at recouping the advantage of specialisation, either through more appropriate targeting of needs or by economies of scale within a narrower area of the market, thereby achieving lower costs.

Porter suggested that *you must choose* which generic strategies you should focus on, and that if you don't, then your strategy will not succeed and you will 'get stuck in the middle.' (Like Rover Group, which aimed to be differentiated in some products, cost leadership in others, covering a wide area of the market and yet sometimes focusing on niches within the organisational structure within different strategic business units.)

The arguments for supporting this prescription are that:

- there are good empirical case studies to support it (like Rover Group).

- culturally, it is very hard to have a differentiation and cost leadership mind-set simultaneously, even where activities are semi-insulated from each other.

The arguments against it are that:

- More flexible operations can sometimes fine-tune the delivery or competitive strategies.

- An organisation may have a mixture of superior value creating competencies (leading to 'motivator factors' (Grundy 1998b, 2002) along with those more basic standards (or the customers' 'hygiene factors'), and that you may therefore just need to juggle these when prioritising how to compete.

Porter has also contributed to our thinking on Strategy and the Internet. Unsurprisingly Porter's thoughts on the Internet were that:

'The five forces would be generally worse, as the Internet made information more freely available (helping buyers, and increasing rivalry). The Internet also, potentially, reduces long-term barriers to entry.'

This meant longer-run margins would not be so good.

But, there might be temporary advantages through simplifying the industry value chain, helping to reduce costs, until customers and competitors bargained that value away.

What are his links to the other gurus?

Porter's work on competitive advantage is very similar to that of Kenichi Ohmae (1982). Also his competitive forces are an extension of Ansoff's environmental scanning (1975). Indeed 'competitive strategy' is a much more powerful and comprehensive model/process than that developed by Ansoff in the 1960s. Porter's five forces are also linked with the author's own idea of 'the industry mind-set' as the underpinning competitive force which Porter missed.

What are his main works?

1 'Competitive Strategy', The Free Press, Macmillan, New York, 1980 – a thorough account of the life-cycle dynamics of industries incorporating the five competitive forces; and of the critical success factors of different phases.

2 'Competitive Advantage', The Free Press, Macmillan, New York, 1985 – Porter's generic strategies and the value chain.

3 'From Competitive Advantage to Corporate Strategy', Harvard Business Review, pp 43-59, May-June 1987 – an account of how acquisitions should be managed for corporate value.

4 'Strategy and the Internet', Harvard Business Review, March-April 2001: an after-the-event analysis of why the Internet has been disappointed in commercial terms.

What are his main concepts?

- Industry life-cycles;
- Porter's five forces;
- the value-chain;
- competitive advantage;
- sustainability;
- the generic strategies; and
- the competitive advantage of nations.

Ease of reading – 'Competitive Advantage' is relatively difficult but well worth it. 'Competitive Strategy' is probably still a 'must read'.

J B Quinn

Who is J B Quinn?

J B Quinn was a major thinker within the process school of strategy. Quinn played a major influence in suggesting that strategic management was not primarily about analytical, rational activity, but was very much dependent upon strategic action. 'Strategic action' means that strategy evolves in a way which is virtually impossible to distinguish from everyday management action.

What is he famous for?

Quinn is famous for explaining how strategic decisions typically evolve in a part random, or erratic, and part logical way. Quinn (1980) coined the expression 'logical incrementalism' to capture this idea. Clearly, strategic decisions did have some logic to them, otherwise strategic action would be foolish, and the business unsuccessful, and top people would get fired. (Having written this in 2002, for a split second this proposition actually seems plausible – after the corporate disasters of the early new millennium, and the resulting stockmarket melt down.) But in the long run top managers are awarded *for not* being foolish, so illogical incrementalism is not really an option.

Whilst being influenced significantly by Braybrooke and Lindblom (1963), Quinn (1980) incorporated within his theory of strategic decisions both random and logical elements.

Quinn's view was that managers tended to make strategic decisions according to perceptions of incremental opportunities which appeared to add to what they already had. Partly driven by their business legacy, and partly by the change, and partly by thirst for incremental profit, top managers were attracted to *piecemeal strategies*.

The practical advantages of logical incrementalism are that:

- Strategic decisions tended to be made on the basis of existing competencies and knowledge, thus reducing exposure.

- By making them incrementally, this made it more possible to digest their implementation (as managers would have to execute strategies before moving on to new ones).

- Their economic value could (in theory) be better targeted, monitored and controlled.

- This style of strategy provided (again, in theory), ample opportunity to learn.

On the downside, the practical disadvantages of logical incrementalism are that:

- Managers would typically not anticipate where a particular decision might lead them next. Like a poor chess player, managers would tend to think about their current move primarily, their next move little, and the one after probably hardly, or not at all.

- Where a series of strategic moves did not necessarily fit together well then over time this would create something of a strategic mess. (Quinn called this 'disjointed incrementation'.)

Quinn's work was very thoroughly researched. In his study of strategic decision-making in major corporations there was ample evidence of logical incrementalism at work. But just as we saw in our discussion of Henry Mintzberg (1994), another (and more famous) strategy guru, just because this is how managers typically do it does not mean that they cannot do it another way. Nor does it mean that they *should not* do it another way.

The authors' personal view (both from empirical research (see Grundy and Brown, 2002) and from over twenty five years business experience managers can benefit from using strategic thinking to manage in a more holistic way. Indeed, when they are shown how to do this, not only are they able to be less incremental but they *certainly want to*. The experience of managers at Lex, John Menzies Group, Oxford University Press, Standard Life, Tesco and many others, testifies to the suggestion that shifts in strategy style towards more holistic thinking are at least partly sustainable.

What are his links to other gurus?

Quinn is closely linked to the process school of strategy, for example with Henry Mintzberg. This school has its roots in organisational decision theory stemming from Braybrooke and Lindblom.

What is his major work?

'Strategies for Change – Logical Incrementalism' Richard D Irwin, Illinois 1980 – is a research based account of patterns in strategic decision-making.

What is his main concept?

Logical incrementation.

Ease of reading – medium.

Alfred Rappaport

Who is Alfred Rappaport?

Alfred Rappaport was a key founder of the Shareholder Value movement. As long ago as the early-mid 1980s he helped lay the foundation for a more explicit focus in strategy formulation for managing it to create shareholder value.

What is he famous for?

Rappaport is most famous for highlighting the need to explore value and cost drivers when attempting to put an (economic) value on a strategy.

A 'value driver' can be defined here as being:

'Anything both within and outside the business, which might directly or indirectly generate case *inflows*, either now or in the future' (Grundy 2002).

A 'cost driver can be defined as being:

'Anything, both within and outside the business, which might directly or indirectly generate cash *outflows*, either now or in the future' (Grundy 2002).

Value and cost drivers are thus quite tangible things.

An example of a value driver in the holiday industry is that of word-of-mouth which will help to generate incremental sales volume without pushing up marketing costs.

An example of a cost driver in the financial services industry is the number of brand managers required per branch. It is not necessary to have a single senior manager to look after a particular branch. On the contrary, one branch-level manager can look after perhaps one or even two branches.

Examples of value drivers and cost drivers for a new, innovative super-market trolley are continued in Figures 17 and Figures 18.

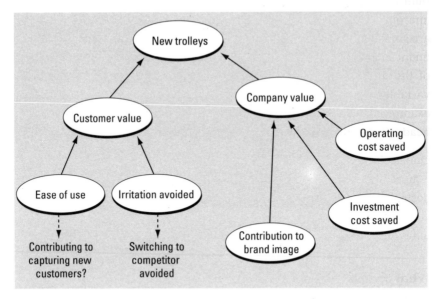

FIGURE 17: VALUE DRIVERS

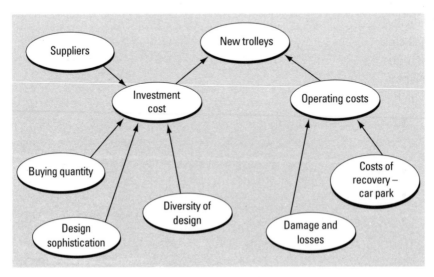

FIGURE 18: COST DRIVERS

Rappaport's own definitions of value and cost drivers are actually much more tangible, and much closer to the direct generation of the financial numbers themselves. For example, Rappaport lists 'sales growth' and 'margin' as 'value drivers'. From the author's viewpoint, these definitions are somewhat limited, as they focus too closely to the directly quantifying financial numbers. Frequently it is more interesting to define them in terms of the underlying system which actually generates these intermediate variables (or Grundy's 'Business Value System' (1998b)) The earlier examples above of 'word-of-mouth' value drivers and 'number of branch heads per branch' for cost drivers are perhaps more useful.

One useful insight from Rappaport, however, is that margin level is often a more important value driver than sales growth. Often growth actually destroys rather than creates shareholder value, especially when the growth is not of particularly high quality (for instance where there is a relatively unfavourable set of Porter's five forces).

What are his links to the other gurus?

McTaggart et al 1994, Reimann, whilst are heavily quantitative and McTaggart et al 1994 and Reimann 1990 are more qualitative, Rappaport falls somewhere in the middle in terms of his relative emphasis on qualitative versus qualitative analysis. Rappaport's stress of margins levels also has close links with Michael Porter's emphasis on the economic analysis of industries. The idea of value creation can be developed even further (for example, by the author 2002) through for instance the value-over-time curve, which can be applied to:

- Corporate strategy.
- Business strategy.
- Implementation.
- Meetings.
- Customer experience and value.

An example of its application to customer experiences and value is shown in Figure 19 – which involves the curtains falling down, the pole damaging the resident, the subsequent pain and the hotel losing the visitor's car keys for a while.

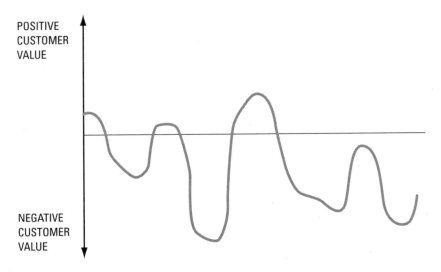

What is his major work?

In 'Creating Shareholder Value', The Free Press, New York 1986, Rappaport gives a comprehensive treatment of the role of value and cost drivers in generating shareholder value.

What is his main concept?

That of value drivers.

Ease of reading – moderately difficult.

Peter Senge (a major guru)

Who is Peter Senge?

Peter Senge is Director of the Systems Thinking and Organizational Learning Program at MIT's Sloan School of Management, and has consulted extensively with major corporations.

What is he famous for?

Peter Senge was famous for the learning organisation. Writing in the early 1990s Senge emphasised the role of learning is not only developing and implementing strategy, but also in managing performance. The 'learning organisation' was intended to signal a shift from thinking about strategic issues as part of a formal, bureaucratic process to its being completely infused with organisational learning.

At the heart of this idea was the concept of 'systems thinking'. For Senge 'systems thinking' meant that one needed to allow free interflow of debate throughout the organisation. This represented a major shift away from being focused on strategic decision-making, centred especially on the top of the organisation – in a hierarchical model. An example of a 'systems thinking picture' used for scenario development is shown in Figure 20.

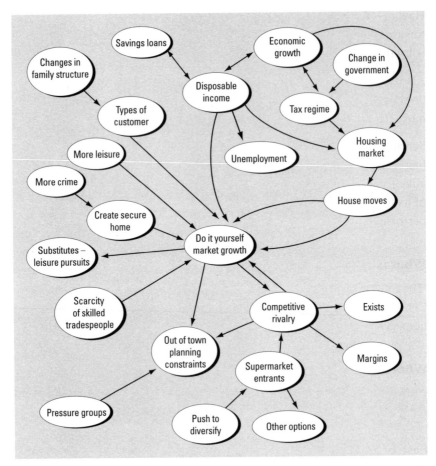

FIGURE 20: SCENARIO DEVELOPMENT

The idea of the 'learning organisation' did become very popular, but in practical terms few companies have actually managed to get the idea taken seriously by top managers.

What are his links to the other gurus?

The author's own research on the Value of Strategic Thinking (Grundy and Brown 2002) suggests that there are still very major organisational constraints to achieve these ambitions.

Having said this, the 'learning organisation' is a useful step on the way towards getting companies to exploit their natural organisational capability (Ulrich 1990) more effectively.

Also, Senge's idea of 'systems thinking' is useful in developing scenarios (Wack 1985), and also in developing Porter's (1985) value chain into something more tailored and interactive – the Business Value System (Grundy 2002).

Senge is most closely linked to process the artist's including Mintzberg who has even gone as far as to suggest that strategic planning is simply unworkable. There are also some links with Kaplan's balance of score-card' in terms of its focus on the softer issues as well as the harder issues in evaluating performance.

What is his main work?

'The Fifth Discipline – The Art and Practise of the Learning Organisation', Century Business, 1990 – which is a patchwork of ideas of how organisations are interactive systems with learning, feedback loops.

What are his main concepts?

- Systems thinking;
- the learning organisation.

Ease of reading – difficult – 'The Fifth Discipline' is not the most accessible book.

A Slyvosky

Who is Slyvosky?

Slyvosky is founding partner of Corporate Decisions, an international strategy consulting company.

What was he famous for?

Slyvosky was famous for the idea of Value Migration. Value Migration is a simple concept which means that businesses often need to reinvent how they add value as industries and their markets change. This might, for example involve:

- Getting rid of activities which add little value, which dilute value, or which destroy value (like Dyson's 'Say goodbye to the bag' in his cyclonic carpet cleaning machine).

- Exploiting new ways of distribution (for example using the Internet, or for the football industry, using new forms of media).

- Rebundling or unbundling existing products or services (for example, the funerals business offers a myriad of different combinations in which value can be added, for example, by services facilitating the do-it-yourself market) see Grundy and Brown 'Be Your Own Strategy Consultant'.

What are his links to other gurus?

- Slyvosky's work has linkages and parallels with:
- Ansoff (1965) – the issue of value migration entails questioning 'what business(es) are you in?'
- Hamel and Prahalad (1994) – 'value migration' is another way of saying competing for the future.
- Hamel and Prahalad's (1990) – core competence (adding new ones).
- Porter's value chain (1985), involving innovation within it.

- Shareholder value theory – finding new ways of creating or capturing customer value (Grundy 1998b).

- Finding new ways of adding distinctive value (or the customer's 'motivator factors' – things that make switching to other sources of supply virtually unthinkable – Grundy 1998, Grundy and Brown 2002).

- Transforming the organisation (Pascale 1990, Peters 1982), and competing from within (Ulrich 1990).

What is his main work?

'Value Migration' contains powerful arguments drawn from specific case studies for not standing still and for continually reinventing yourself.

What is his main concept?

Value migration.

Ease of reading – relatively easy – a good and stimulating read.

J C Spender

Who is J C Spender?

J C Spender is Professor of Strategic Management at Strathclyde University.

What is he famous for?

Spender is famous for his concept of 'strategic recipes.' Strategic recipes are the taken-for-granted rules of strategic decision-making which characterise the strategic action of the top team.

Strategic recipes are founded on things that have worked, or not worked in the past. These recipes relate back to a past group, or individual, strategic situations. When a new leader is appointed, particularly from the outside these are likely to change – or at least be challenged. Besides company level recipes, we can expand this notion to look at (strategic) industry recipes, a very similar idea to the author's own concept of 'the industry mind-set'. Another refinement (see Grundy 1992) is to couple these with 'financial recipes', which capture the decision criteria/the worst of situations where a company believes it has made money in the past, or will make money in the future.

What are his links to other gurus?

Spencer is associated with Mintzberg's emergent strategy, with strategic recipes guiding the choice of strategic option, rather than formal, strategic analysis.

What is his major work?

'Strategy Making in Business', PhD, University of Massachusetts, 1980.

What is his main concept?

Strategic recipes.

Ease of reading – medium.

E Stalk

Who is Stalk?

Stalk is a writer who realised that Ohmae/Porter's concepts of 'competitive advantage' appeared rather static, and did not take into account the edge which can come through momentum through time.

What was Stalk famous for?

Stalk was famous for putting the idea of 'competitive advantage' into a more dynamic context, notably by incorporating the dimension of time.

More specifically, Stalk emphasised the role which *speed* played in determining competitive advantage. As conventional paths to competitive advantage (differentiation, cost leadership, focus, core and distinctive competencies) could often be copied, Stalk suggested that *speed* was an important path to competitive advantage work, in its own right.

By 'speed' Stalk meant:

- The rate of competitive innovation: being able to innovate faster than your competitors.
- The speed with which strategic opportunities are identified and exploited.
- The speed of implementation.
- Responsiveness to customer need (at a transaction-by-transaction level).

What are his main links to other gurus?

His main links are to Porter (generic strategies, 1985), Hamel and Prahalad (1994) (competing for the future) and Ohmae 1982 (the three 'C's').

What is his main work?

'Competing Against Time', The Free Press, Macmillan, 1990, is a lucid account of how time-based competition (as Stalk calls it) can be created and sustained.

What is his main concept?

Time-based competition.

Ease of reading – relatively easy.

Sun Tzu (a major guru, now deceased)

Who was Sun Tzu?

Sun Tzu was an ancient Chinese military theorists who was one of the very earliest strategists.

What was he famous for?

Sun Tzu was famous for his discussion of the strategic lessons which need to be applied in situations of conflict. These lessons deal with the imperatives of strategic choice, focus, and of dominance.

One of Sun Tzu's recommendations is that strategy development should *begin* with the victory scene. What does this scene actually look like? How many people are still alive, dead or injured, who do they belong to, and who has emerged as the victor? How was victory brought about, what was the context of the battle, and what actually led up to this?

As you can easily see this approach entails working backwards from your desired result, what is sometimes called (Grundy 2002) the 'Spice Girl Strategy' or 'what is it that you really, really, want?'. It also involves a story telling approach – very similar to that required to do effective scenario development. But the author's favourite quote from Sun Tzu is:

> *'When the front is prepared the rear is unprepared. And when the rear is prepared then the front is unprepared. Preparedness on the right means a lack on the left. And preparedness on the left means a lack on the right.*
>
> *But preparedness everywhere means a lack everywhere.'*

This is good to enact in workshops by pretending to physically do the various manoeuvres (a largish room is pretty essential for this).

The above quote is very powerful and is an important lesson to strategists everywhere. It is especially important at the corporate strategy level, where resources are often dissipated across too many (and too diverse) strategic business units. Indeed each Chief Executive should have the above quote nailed facing his or her desk, and probably as an automatic prompt on their lap-tops as well!

Who is linked to Sun Tzu?

Michael Porter's 'Competitive Advantage' is an obvious candidate, being a guru who is in the Sun Tzu mode. But many of Sun Tzu's military anecdotes/lessons are also reminiscent of Mintzberg's emergent strategy and the process school. This is also linked to the author's notion of 'conditional strategy'.

What is his major work?

'The Art of War' Sun Tzu – a tapestry of suggestions about how to seize advantage.

What is his major concept?

- Dominance;
- strategic intent;
- resource-based competitive advantage;
- capability.

Ease of reading – easy – but you do need to think a lot!

David Ulrich (a major guru)

Who is David Ulrich?

David Ulrich teaches at the University of Michigan. (See also Welch 2001.) He was a major force behind 'Work-Out', GE's culture change programme. He has consulted with many multinational companies.

What is he famous for?

David Ulrich is famous for looking at how organisations can create competitive advantage from the inside-out and not from the outside-in (or from a competitive strategy standpoint). Ulrich's thinking is closely designed with the idea of 'resource-based' competitive advantage (Grant 1991). In this perspective, the most central insights on strategy are held to come out of an analysis of a company's resource base, and not from its competitive market place.

Ulrich takes this idea one stage further by suggesting that the softer aspects of the resource base – the organisation – are actually central in understanding competitive position. This view corresponds with many of the author's observations over the years. For example, when he spoke to a major supplier to Tesco about a client of his, the (then) Director of Non-Food at Tesco, Simon Uwins, said:

> "Oh, you know Simon Uwins, a great guy. Actually, Simon would never have the same job at Sainsbury's. No, I correct myself, he would not even be employed by Sainsbury."

This was obviously a reflection of the perceived differences in culture (and in organisational effectiveness) perceived by this person at the time between Tesco and Sainsbury, and was not a slur in any way on Simon's effectiveness.

David Ulrich's second major contribution to strategy was that of his emphasis on HR's role as being more than that of consultant/facilitator, rather than as Personnel Administration. Ulrich saw HR as potentially being there to facilitate the implementation of business strategy, and also, potentially of its formulation too. Sadly, whilst much hype exists on HR circles about the changing role, few HR staff appear to a) fully understand it, b) be capable of executing that role.

What are his links to other gurus?

Ulrich is an organisational development turned organisational strategist. Accordingly, he falls into a similar school of thought to Argyris (1991), Handy (1994), Kanter (1983) Mintzberg (1994), Pascale (1990), Peters (1982) and Senge (1990). A more recent text is Grundy and Brown (2003 – forthcoming).

What is his main work?

'Organizational Capability – Competing from the Inside Out', John Wiley & Sons, New York, 1990 – summarises his main arguments very effectively.

What are his major concepts?

- HR strategy;
- capability.

Ease of reading – medium.

P Wack

Who is Wack?

Wack is a former senior strategic planner at Shell during the period when Shell was using scenario development to anticipate major and unexpected shifts in the business environment.

What was he famous for?

Wack was instrumental in promoting the idea of scenario development not just within Shell but to the outside world as well. One of Shell's notable successes with scenarios as a process of story-telling was in anticipating the oil crisis of the 1970s.

Not only did Shell anticipate this disruptive event but also had contingency strategies in place for dealing with it. This, it was deemed, allowed to react much faster than its competitors – the other oil company majors of that time. Scenario story-telling is a dynamic process which can be understood better through the author's own 'uncertainty tunnel' (see Figure 21). This helps think through the force and volatility of a change, and of the series of its likely effects.

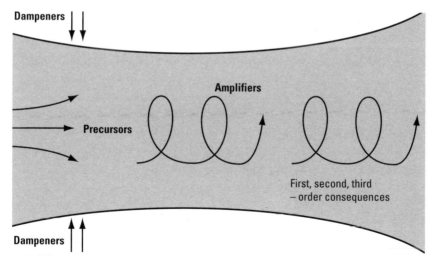

FIGURE 21: THE UNCERTAINTY TUNNEL

Scenario story-telling is a fluid process, possibly drawing from PEST factors, the growth drivers and Porter's five forces. But it is also helped considerably by using Mitroff's uncertainty-importance grid, as used also by Shell (see Figure 13).

Companies where the uncertainty-importance grid has now been introduced, coupled with scenario development include: Amerada Petroleum, BT, Direct Line, HSBC, Standard Life and Tesco.

What are his links to other gurus?

Wack (and his ex-Shell colleagues including De Geus (1988) – many of whom have now become strategy academics) have close links to Hamel and Prahalad (1994) ('Competing for the Future'), Argyris (double-loop learning 1991), and Senge (1990) (the learning organisation/systems thinking). Scenarios are also used as a vehicle for sensing, amplifying and interpreting weak environmental signals – (Ansoff 1975).

What are his main works?

1   Scenarios – 'Unchartered Waters Ahead', Harvard Business Review, pp 73-89 September-October 1985.

2   Scenarios – 'Shooting the Rapids', Harvard Business Review, pp139-150, November-December 1985.

What are his major concepts?

- Discontinuities;
- scenarios;
- transitional events.

Ease of reading – relatively easy.

Jack Welch (a major guru)

Who is Jack Welch?

Jack Welch was the Chairman of General Electric (GE), once called 'the greatest manager of the twentieth century'.

What was he famous for?

Jack Welch was responsible for initiating 'Work-Out' which involved problem-solving within every level of the work force.

Welch also pioneered the first real downsizing in the US in the 1980s, simultaneously with implementing a cultural revolution in the organisation.

Welch's focus on ideas generation and dissemination extended to the use of total quality management, and preparation for the Internet-based organisation. Indeed, GE is perhaps one of the very few real examples of the learning organisation.

Welch, perhaps above all, embodied Hamel and Prahalad's idea of 'strategy as stretch', being awesome in his challenging style.

How does he link to the other gurus?

Welch has played a major influence in the work of Kanter (1983) ('The Change Masters'), Pascale ('Managing on the Edge') (1990), Peters ('Thriving on Chaos') (1987) and Senge (1990) ('The Learning Organisation').

What is his main work?

'Jack: Straight from the Gut', Warner Inc, New York, 2001: this is an intense, personal account of his experiences in transforming GE.

What are his major concepts?

- The learning organisation;
- downsizing;
- delayering;
- organisational transformation.

Ease of reading – easy.

George Yip

Who is George Yip?

George Yip has taught at Harvard, the University of California and was also Professor of Strategic Management at Cambridge University. He is also a consultant to leading corporations.

What was he famous for?

George Yip's 'Total Global Strategy' is a standard text on global strategy on many leading MBA courses. His book helps us to discriminate between the extent to which markets are truly global, by looking at different drivers, including:

- Market drivers.
- Competitive drivers.
- Cost drivers.
- Governmental drivers.

He also looks at the cost/benefits of being global, across products and services, marketing, competitive moves, and organisation. Rare for more US-based thinking (originally), he is less prescriptive in his views, taking a more diagnostic view of the otherwise cloudy concept of 'global' – and also taking a contingency approach to its applicability (i.e. being 'global' depends on the context).

What is his main work?

'Total Global Strategy', Prentice Hall, Englewood Cliffs, 1992.

What are his main concepts?

Global strategy.

Ease of reading – reasonably difficult, due to the detail.

FOUR
Champney's health resort and the business strategy gurus

Introduction

Let us now turn to a case study which illustrates the relevance of the strategy gurus (mentioned in brackets) and is based on a documentary on BBC television in 1996 and also on interviews with Champney's Managing Director. This case illustrates:

- Acquisitions
- Breakthroughs
- Competitive advantage
- Competitive positioning
- Competitive strategy
- Cost drivers
- Deliberate and emergent strategies
- Differentiation
- Divestment
- Future thinking
- HR strategy
- Integration
- Legacy

- Logical incrementation
- Marketing strategy
- Mission
- Paradigms
- Options
- Shared values
- Stakeholders
- Stakeholder value
- Strategic fit
- Strategic change
- Strategic leadership
- Strategic intent.

Background

Champney's Health Farm is located at Tring, Hertfordshire, UK. Champney's is a select, rural retreat for its members who reside principally in and around the Home Counties, England. Traditionally it is a most exclusive retreat, charging near-Savoy prices for its luxurious and relatively exotic services – in body and skin care generally.

But by the recession of the 1990s Champney's was suffering considerably. Falling demand meant that its cash flow had deteriorated to the point where it experienced an annual cash deficit of one million pounds. Its previous owners decided that enough was enough, and sold out to foreign investors *(acquisitions)*.

In business terms, Champney's was in dire need of strategic change (Johnson and Scholes, Kanter), no longer having *strategic fit* to the environment. So its new, foreign investors decided that a new breath of life needed to be injected – to secure Champney's future.

In late 1995, Savoy trained Lord Thurso was recruited to spearhead Champney's recovery. It had been recently acquired by a new Middle Eastern owner who it would appear existed after the acquisition, needed an *integration strategy*. (Haspelagh and Jemison.) As its new Chief Executive, Lord Thurso set about formulating a turnaround plan which would secure Champney's a viable future. At this time Champney's also featured on a BBC2 production, 'Trouble at the Top'. Some of the quotes by Lord Thurso are taken from that television programme and some from interviews with one of the authors.

Because Champney's prided itself on its exclusive customer service, this turnaround strategy needed to be managed with great sensitivity to the people issues. (Peters, Ulrich and Lake.)

This case study is structured along Johnson and Scholes three phases of strategic management: analysis, choice, and implementation.

Strategic analysis

In the tradition of turnaround specialists, Lord Thurso set himself a tight deadline to formulate and project manage his strategic turnaround plan. This was just one month. In the course of that month Lord Thurso was to spend the bulk of his time listening to Champney's various stakeholders, (Piercy) particularly:

- its members, and regular customers;
- its staff; and
- its current managers.

A number of *strategic breakthroughs* were born out of Lord Thurso's strategic thinking as follows:

- Sampling Champney's treatments (by Lord Thurso).
- Simplifying management processes.
- Improving management reporting processes.
- Management restructuring.
- Management recruitment.
- The communication plan.
- The strategic vision.
- Developing a business strategy.
- Customer database.
- Maintaining organisational morale.
- Culture change.
- Getting rid of Health-for-Life.
- Premises strategy.
- The business case and its approval.

To begin with, when Lord Thurso took over Champney's he weighed in at 16 stones. As a parallel agenda, Lord Thurso undertook to reduce this weight – coincidentally in parallel with what became Champney's own corporate slimming exercise. Most important in those early days for Lord Thurso was to sample Champney's exotic, health-generating treatments, being his first project to help turn the business round, in order to understand customer value delivered and *competitive advantage* (Ohmae, Porter).

Lord Thurso's early diagnosis within the turnaround project indicated that Champney's suffered from a number of underlying legacy problems, including:

- A *legacy* of under-investment (and decay), due to past *shareholder value* destruction (Rappaport).
- A decline in standards generally.
- An over-zealous attempt to market Champney's time-shares – to customers outside Champney's core customer base (this was an inappropriate deliberate strategy, Mintzberg).
- Promises made to members which could not be kept.
- A top-heavy management structure (which was a major *cost driver*, rather than a lean one (Peters), and a lack of *strategic leadership*.
- Relatively poor (or inappropriate) management and financial controls.
- A lack of sense of strategic direction generally.

Champney's difficult situation was brought about by a combination of unrealistic past *deliberate strategy* (Mintzberg), a lack of *organisational alignment* (Peters and Waterman, Senge, Ulrich and Lake) and *muddling through* and *incremental thinking* (Braybrooke and Lindblom, Quinn).

Lord Thurso wisely negotiated a remuneration package which would not disadvantage him in recommending possibly unpalatable options – highlighting the linkages between strategic thinking, reward structure, and *shareholder value* (McTaggart et al).

Reflecting on this situation (in an interview in 2000), on the strategic choices available (Johnson and Scholes), Lord Thurso elaborates:

"There isn't any money and my job is to get the value out – bang, bang, bang. They take difficult decisions with easy. In a way, what I was doing was not far short of that. You arrive, the thing is absolutely bleeding to

death and the shareholders are not going to be able to bale it out a great deal more and you have to have a plan for dealing with the emergency situation.

That's when you whip the patient into an ambulance and off to hospital.

The thing was absolutely in the shit – that is a technical term."

Lord Thurso continued:

"When I first started I had an option, which was to recommend closing the business down, and I would be paid, I would have a kind of parachute, so I was free to say: 'Look, I am sorry, I don't feel that the business is viable, the only way out is to chop it up and sell all the bits off...'" [recaps on the process during the first months].

Lord Thurso, on his first inspection of the property after taking over tells us (BBC2):

"It is clearly very tired. These rooms would have been considered five star when they were built but clearly the expectations of five star has changed. It is bland, it is grey, it is a very dead, dull room, it has no colour and it has zero on the excitement scale."

Also, Champney's strategic positioning (Ansoff, Porter) itself seemed to be unclear and its marketing strategy:

"I have asked the question of everybody 'what are we selling?' and I get a lot of long-winded answers; the real answer is that no-one has thought about it." (BBC2)

He also reflects (1997 interview):

"I had also decided – it was as plain as day that the previous strategy, there was this wonderful name 'Champney's', which is true, it is the great opportunity. But what had been created in the past was the infrastructure for a hundred million pound company even though it was only a ten million pound company.

It had all these people here who were called brand managers. And none of them understood what a brand was. And that was the extraordinary thing. None of them understood the elementary concept of a brand being a promise made to customers that has values and a character. If you said to them 'what does Champney's mean?' – the answer was, they hadn't thought it through."

Whilst Champney's thought it had a deliberate strategy, it was probably more emergent (Mintzberg) indicating the kind of bureaucracy which Peters and Waterman twenty years ago suggested was irrelevant. Many of these issues must have been apparent almost as soon as Lord Thurso drove up Champney's drive. As soon as he arrived he found a mass of memos from his managers. Lord Thurso says (BBC2):

"There are piles and piles of paper. It is a fairly classic thing. There are too many managers sending memos to each other. And I am suspicious of any company that is capable of generating so much paper when they are told they are expecting a new Chief Executive."

Also (1997 interview):

"When I arrived here there were huge reports on everything. I said to them, 'Look I just don't read them. I don't mind reading a novel by Tolstoy or Dick Francis, but I am not going to read that!"

The following reveals Lord Thurso's quite different management style which was one of leadership (Pascale):

"I tend to communicate by getting up and sitting in someone's office. I loathe memos. In my last company I banned them completely for two months. I said 'the next person who writes a memo will be fired' – it was amazing, we didn't have a single memo written for two months. It was brilliant, people actually started talking to one another." (1997 interview)

The above thinking clearly flagged-up two significant strategic breakthroughs – simplifying management processes and improving management reporting processes.

At the same time management lacked the fundamental information that it required for managing *shareholder value* – it was based on inappropriate accounting data (BBC2):

> "We do not have good financial information, in fact not only is it not good it is actually awful. The management accounts that I have seen are mathematically correct but they are not informative."

So, besides simplifying the management process, a further strategic break-through would need to be improving management reporting processes.

He continued on structure (Chandler, Handy, Mintzberg, Peters):

> "There was a management structure which didn't work. The management reports were gibberish. I asked simple questions – 'Do you know what your cash flow is?' and the guy couldn't tell me... They didn't produce balance sheets. They produced huge, thick reports, full of graphs, trend analysis. But the one thing that they didn't do was to produce reports where you could find profit, where you could find cash flow. I said we will really have to start from scratch.

> I remember sitting on the lawn on holiday wearing my Panama hat and a tee-shirt and my kilt, and smoking a cigar trying to read through two years of drivel, the management accounts... I can usually work things out and I just couldn't make it work."

But instead of rolling out a strategic turnaround plan straight away, Lord Thurso spent precious time soliciting the views of all its key stakeholders, especially of its disgruntled customers – focusing on diagnosis (Johnson and Scholes). This enabled him not only to be absolutely sure that his chosen path was the right one – in deliberate strategy terms but also, in behavioural terms, was owned (Kanter), and didn't produce a reaction due to the organisation's *shared values.*

This period of listening was primarily so Lord Thurso could establish a rapport with his new staff and thus to provide a platform for influencing them effectively. He told me:

> "To be honest, I had already made up my mind before I arrived here what I would do. I had actually decided before the day that I started that I was going to take a million pounds out of the costs." (1997 interview)

He continued:

> "I wanted them to have thought that I had thought it through. They wouldn't have understood that I was capable of thinking it through very quickly, and that it was really clear what had to be done. It was really a very simple problem and it needed some pretty straightforward solutions.
>
> After I arrived I said 'I will have a month and I will take no decisions until the end of the month'. It was a good thing. I did fractionally amend certain decisions but ninety per cent of it was exactly what I had thought (previously)." (1997 interview)

Strategic thinking does not necessarily need a lot of time to accomplish – unlike Mintzberg's characterisation of it with his attack in 'The Rise and Fall of Strategic Planning'. Nevertheless it is important to ensure that parallel strategic thinking occurs, even at a simplified level and at a slower speed in the rest of the organisation. This does not come naturally easily to those senior managers who are particularly bright.

Lord Thurso realised intuitively that Champney's was the kind of situation which could so easily blow up if a number of *stakeholders* (Piercy) decided, rightly or wrongly, that he was 'the wrong man for the job'. Quite quickly Lord Thurso concluded from his own personal course of treatments that his operational staff were a real asset – to be retained, nurtured and grown. Lord Thurso said:

> "The closer I get to the front line the better I find the troops are. And that is very pleasing because if you have good officers and lousy soldiers you have got a lot of work to do, but if you have good soldiers and lousy officers, then you have to work to train or change the officers." (BBC2)

In some contrast, Lord Thurso found the management which he inherited, although up to the task of managing in a more steady state environment, not really up to a turnaround. The top-heavy management structure was not only an expense that the business could not afford; it also impeded the recovery plan, inviting two further interrelated breakthroughs – management restructuring and management recruitment.

Lord Thurso reflects in late 1997 just how serious the problems at the old 'Head Office' had become:

> "And there was a business over there that had been completely neglected at Head Office. There was a flipchart in every office, which to me was a symptom of this very introverted style – the moment anybody had a meeting someone was on a flipchart. The whole thing was driven by the processes rather than by the objectives. If there were objectives they were tacked onto the process."

> People worked hard and interacted and interfaced and essentially went around in circles. There was no questioning of 'why are we here?' or 'What is the meaning of the universe?'

> It was quite clear that I had to make a very clear, that I had to make a very definitive statement that there was a complete change coming. It wasn't quite as bloody as it looked, because I re-deployed quite a lot of the people I had here back into the units. That refocused them on where the action was.

> I described it once as 'this Head Office was once a great black hole which sucked energy out of the units. Things vanished into it never to be seen again'. Whereas my idea of Head Offices is that it should be a tiny, tiny star in the sky, twinkling light down, completely out of the way." (Interview)

Here Lord Thurso is giving a steer on the value-adding activities of the *corporate centre* (Campbell and Goold.), and is using contention deliberately (Pascale).

Strategic choice

As Lord Thurso said (illustrating Senge's systems thinking) (interview 2000):

"I think life is all about circles and not straight lines. You can jump onto the circle anywhere you like. Number one, it is having a vision – call it a vision, call it an objective, call it a goal, it is the idea of where you want to go. The beginning of strategic thinking is where you are working out the vision strategy, then it's mapping out the ways in which you could deliver that, like policies you put in place. Overall, a series of moves in chess is a strategy. Each move is a tactic."

He continues, on the role of leadership and vision, or strategic intent (Peters, Hamel and Prahalad):

"The leader has to ensure that there is a vision, that there is a clear idea. Whether the leader dreams that idea up himself or whether that idea is produced by a process of consultation, it doesn't really matter. He then has to make sure that there is a strategy for prosecuting it."

At this point it is now worthwhile doing an exercise on what you would see as being the possible *strategic options* facing Champney's.

This can be done at three levels:

1   Options for competitive strategy – *competitive positioning* (Ansoff, Ohmae, Porter).

2   Options for organisational (or 'HR') strategy (Ulrich and Lake).

3   Options for the change process (Kanter, Pascale).

To help you to think about level 1) consider once again the following 'lines of enquiry': these are depicted as the 'Octopus' or 'Option Octopus' (Grundy 2002) which is an extension of the Ansoff grid (see Figure 22):

* Which market sectors should Champney's be in?

* Where? (Geographic options.)

* Which customers should it target and what areas of value creation? (Rappaport, Grundy.)

- Are there different means of value delivery and resource bases?

- Are there alliance or acquisition possibilities? (Haspeslagh and Jemison, Lorange and Roos.)

- Might Champney's divest or outsource any activities as a group? (Campbell and Goold.)

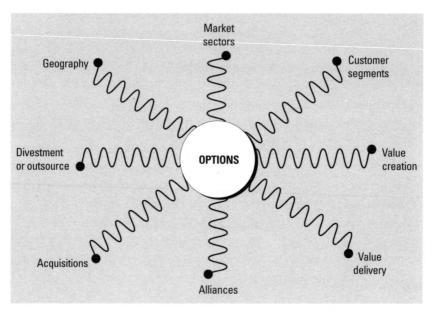

FIGURE 22: OCTOPUS

Here we see the need to be quite creative and fluid in your strategic thinking. As Lord Thurso reflects (interview, 2000): *future thinking* "The guy at the top must always be mentally in the future."

EXERCISE

Champney's – options for competitive strategy

Based on the case study so far, your imagination, and upon structured input from the 'Octopus':

- What key strategic options can you think of for Champney's?

- How attractive are they on the Strategic Option Grid (using the scoring techniques of three ticks means very attractive, two ticks means average attractiveness, and one tick means low attractiveness)? (See Chapter 1.)

- What overall scores do you get for the various options?

- Can you think of any ways of making these options more attractive (through the 'cunning plan', Blackadder)?

- What key vulnerabilities might reduce your option scores? (Mitroff)

Note: a number of suggestions of possible answers are contained later in this book, somewhere, but it is advisable not to peep at these first.

This kind of reflection needs to be done in some specially created thought or 'helicopter' space (and time) (for strategic thinking (Mintzberg). Lord Thurso reflected (interview, 2000), illustrating that:

> "The guy at the top is probably the only person spending his time thinking six to nine months ahead of the business. The most important single thing is thinking ahead. The first thing is one, with door shut, with phone switched off, gazing at this ceiling, running 'what-ifs' through my mind..."

Turning now to the organisational structure (which will facilitate the strategy – Chandler), assuming that you are going to reposition Champney's back to its traditional up-market focus, what future organisation would you 'really, really want'.

Implementation

But knowing this posed a major dilemma for Lord Thurso if he were to move very fast and introduce a new, slimmed down management structure, the shock might topple the organisation, undermining morale at the cutting edge of customer service. In these situations there is probably no single 'right answer'. Arguably, by leaving the Champney's managers in suspense for one month, he prolonged the agony of uncertainty. But on the other hand, by at least listening to them over this period he would have a better idea of who was, and was not, able to make the transition – and also how many managers in simple, financial terms, he could take with him.

He continues (interview, 1997) highlighting the need to create some sense of crisis (Pascale, Senge):

"First of all I wanted a huge change and I wanted that to sink in quickly. I wanted the troops, the army in the resort to go 'Hey this guy might know what he is talking about'!

I also felt that I only wanted to do it once. I wanted it to be viciously quick for two reasons, one was to make a point and the other thing was to say to people 'that's it. It is done.' And that undoubtedly worked."

Lord Thurso decided that Champney's above all needed a new strategic vision. (Hamel and Prahalad).

Strategic vision

Lord Thurso's own *vision* for Champney's is profoundly simple. Lord Thurso prefers the idea of 'vision' to 'mission' principally because mission statements are harder to grasp onto, particularly in terms of the behaviours which are implied by them (1997 Interview) (Campbell et al):

> *"If you cannot remember a mission statement (I cannot remember our old one), if you have to refer to something, that's wrong. To me, any mission statement which is 'we will have care for our customers, be nice to our staff, be nice to grey squirrels on Sundays', you know, you have gone to sleep.*

> *It has got to be something that encapsulated the spirit. 'Nowhere else makes you this good (Champney's)' – yes, it is a spirit statement. That's why, NASA says: 'To get a man on the moon' makes sense. At Champney's it is: 'Nowhere else makes you feel this good' – and that should apply to the staff as well."*

Potentially, Lord Thurso faced major resistance to his plan, (and these defensive routines (Argyris, Kanter) especially from his senior managers who expressed their loyalty to their previous MD and to his past strategy (during the television documentary). In business terms there was little alternative but to severely reduce the number of his central management team. Lord Thurso addressed the team at a management meeting (BBC2):

> *"Please view my arrival not as something disastrous but actually as an expression of support by our shareholders.*

> *The problem in a nutshell is that we are losing money. You are all intelligent people and therefore you will know that there will be a cost-cutting exercise. We have an expression in the fitness centre of 'no pain, no gain' but there will be pain.*

> *We are with the cost of Head Office losing as a company approximately one million pounds in cash terms per year. It is my intention and target that by the end of the next year we will be cash-breakeven. The direction I have decided to follow is to put Champney's absolutely and without doubt at the top of the tree."*

He had decided to tell them collectively of his decision so that he delivered two clear and separate messages. The first message was that there was an impelling need to restructure and reduce the management resource, effectively downsizing (Kanter, Peters). The second message was to specific individuals – that they were, or were not, to be members of the future team. Within the restructuring project there would be two sub-projects – diagnosing current skills and defining the future skills needed to deliver the strategy. Indeed, besides developing an overall strategic vision, a further project was also required – developing a business strategy. Key sub-parts of this strategic project were: a marketing strategy for current activities, a review of wider strategic options, a customer services strategy, and finally a premises strategy. This was also related to a further strategic project: to enhance Champney's customer database.

The key factors which needed to line up to deliver the vision of Champney's financial turnaround through 'nowhere else makes you feel this good' were:

- Restructuring and cost reduction.
- Appropriate business strategy.
- Promises now fulfilled – through exit from health for life.
- New management team.
- Staff enthused.
- Financial support for development.
- Appropriate investment.
- Word-of-mouth (resumes).*
- No major adverse environmental change.**

*   factors over which Champney's had partial influence.

**   factors over which Champney's had relatively little influence.

The final alignment factor – no major adverse *environment change* – could be analysed down and positioned separately on the uncertainty grid, particularly for: no increase in competition, substitutes not being a major threat, no major economic stagnation after 2000 etc. (Johnson and Scholes.)

Coming now to Champney's change process, Lord Thurso had a number of *options* in communicating his strategy. One alternative, for instance, would have been to speak to individuals separately – both to communicate the need for the change and whether or not they still had a job. This alternative approach would have had the merit of removing the period of uncertainty during which his managers would have been concerned about their job security. But equally it would have meant that whilst Lord Thurso was interviewing his managers some would have heard about the organisational change sooner than the others.

These simple logistics highlight the behavioural implications (Argyris) of making a *strategic change* in an organisation. For whichever way Lord Thurso played it, the effect on individuals' feelings – perhaps of hurt and fear might have ramifications in their future and also that of the remaining team. Thinking through options in this area is always a major area for applying strategic thinking.

The impact of these redundancies was obviously severe on the managers. Champney's Property Manager, Willie Serplis, attempted to put a brave face on it as he came smiling to the television interview following his meeting with Lord Thurso. His smile quickly faded as he tells us (BBC2):

> *"Do you want to ask the question then... 'How are you?' 'Not very happy. I just lost my job which is better knowing but what can I do? You want to be angry with someone or something but it doesn't make sense. You can dress it up in all the esoteric bullshit you know – downsizing, redundancy – but the reality is, for no fault of my own I have just been fired..."*

Lord Thurso himself looked emotionally strained when he was asked how he felt about this part of the process, showing that it is draining to be a 'Change Master' (Kanter):

> *"I would find it hard to sleep if I felt that anything I was doing was wrong in any way. I dislike doing it, but it is a necessary operation that has to be done on the company. All that one can do is to do it as humanely and professionally as one can.*
>
> *Most of them have been angry because at the end of the day we all like to think that we have a value in an organisation and effectively when*

you are made redundant someone is saying that you don't have a value in the organisation. When I say that it isn't to do with your performance it is to entirely do with the financial structure of the company, it actually doesn't help them very much." (BBC2)

One can imagine the atmosphere within the Management Block at Champney's as the reality sank in that it was the end of an era. Also those staying realised that they would be expected to achieve a quantum shift in the level of effectiveness – if the business were to come back into profit.

The above account highlights a further, short-term project: maintaining organisational morale (Ulrich and Lake).

It was then Lord Thurso's turn to address his operational staff. Lord Thurso appeared to be in a lighter mood as he informed his staff not merely about the severity of the situation but also of the fact that he was not planning other job cuts. He continued:

"The last part of the strategy and the bit that does concern all of you is that New Court and the concept of a headquarters is going to be quite radically scaled down. There are twenty-two people sitting here and we have probably half that for the number of places that I actually have available. You are intelligent and you will have worked this out. And therefore some people are going to have to be made redundant... And I do recognise the pain that this will cause you. I am sorry that some of you will be going, but please understand that it is nothing to do with you and your capability. It is simply about how this business has been run over the past few years and the requirement to put it on a proper cash footing."

In order to restore a viable *differentiation strategy* (Porter) he tries to give staff a stretching vision:

"Finally, I would like to give you a little thought. All my life I have been involved in giving first-class service to people and I believe it is a wonderful thing to do. Be always ready to say 'yes' whenever a client or guest comes to see you and asks for something and you are tempted to say 'no'. Stop, think, and that will help us to create a level of service unheard of in this country."

Besides dealing with internal *stakeholders* (Piercy), Lord Thurso had to manage the expectations of the Champney's members, whose business was needed to secure a successful future. These members had been disappointed in the past by its prior management who had, perhaps, set up expectations about improvements in standards that had not, or could not have, been delivered. Lord Thurso then decided to end the previous management's scheme for time-sharing not only to those sales activities but also to buying-back the time-share. Getting out of this business area proved to be one of the most difficult projects.

Lord Thurso was quick to realise that 'the Health-For-Life' time-sharing scheme, which was a *diversification*, needed to be halted (BBC2) as it was value destroying (Rappaport, Reimann, Grundy):

> "From what I have seen the constant push-push-push on 'Health-For-Life' has given the wrong impression in the marketplace. I think maybe we should cut that right back."

Apparently this was an issue which emerged only during his fact-finding. After being assured by his senior managers that there were not any other burning issues to be brought to his attention ("other than the cash flow", said his finance director) he discovered that (interview, 2000):

> "Some of the key issues I did not realise until later. The fact that the time-share was totally critical and I would need to do that was something which I didn't realise. When I first got here one thought 'yes, that's a time-share business I will have to rev it up'."

He also determined that the physical facilities and amenities at Champney's (its hard to imitate, superior resources – Grant) did not provide a sustainable foundation for its future marketing strategy which was aimed at repositioning Champney's as an exclusive resort (BBC2):

> "What a great architect friend of mine once described as the 'wow' factor. What we have got here is the 'er' factor. What we need is a 'wow' factor."

So, besides the organisational changes which Lord Thurso instigated, he also set about developing an ambitious project to revitalise the physical fabric of Champney's to restore its competitive advantage (Porter). This included:

- A major upgrade in the entrance and facade to the central building – and to the driveway itself.

- A possible conversion of the Management Block to produce twenty additional treatment rooms. This, Lord Thurso hoped, would provide the spur to expand Champney's customers.

These renovations, Lord Thurso hoped, would provide a further benefit, signalling to Champney's employees that Champney's was genuinely going to be set on the road to a prosperous future.

Champney's strategic breakthroughs

But to achieve these plans, Lord Thurso needed to build the confidence of his investors, who might well have thought that a turnaround was not possible without major investment of this order. To achieve this he needed to produce a robust business case which, yet again, became a key project. Lord Thurso realised that to provide the basis for this confidence he would need to achieve a number of things:

- The restructuring of management had to be implemented successfully (Kanter).

- Better financial planning and control needed to be implemented – with the help of its new Finance Director whom Lord Thurso had brought in.

- Lord Thurso's restructuring would need to have delivered the required cost savings.

- Although a *gap* still remained (Ansoff) (to break-even) with these cost savings, this gap would need to be closed by expanding revenues.

- To achieve this, the quality of service and standards generally at Champney's had to improve considerably – to the point where members felt a real difference and new members were brought in (Porter – *a differentiation strategy*).

Although cost savings of half a million pounds per annum were achieved relatively quickly, it proved much slower to improve sales through improving customer confidence. But within one year Champney's managed to break-even. So, Lord Thurso was able to then put into effect his plan to obtain enough investment to reposition Champney's as an outstanding health resort.

The overseas investors were able to give Lord Thurso the vote of confidence he needed in order to move onto Stage Two of the turnaround – a major upgrading programme – whose implementation became a further strategic breakthrough. So, at last, all the planks of Lord Thurso's future strategy were in place.

We have now told the story of Champney's strategic change (Johnson and Scholes) – but mainly from the point of view of the business. But if we look at this situation from a more behavioural point of view, we find that this dimension has perhaps even more importance than more tangible areas of change.

Implementing the strategic breakthroughs

The key three strategic breakthroughs for Champney's comprised:

- the new strategy;
- an effective resource base; and
- a responsive organisation.

We will see these fleshed out in a later section, which summarises the key strategic projects.

The key forces enabling Champney's change programme included Lord Thurso's leadership, the clarity of the strategy, and the support of lower-level operational staff. The most important forces were thus more behavioural in nature. These highlighted that:

- Lord Thurso had introduced a number of key enablers (Lewin) into the strategic change through his own leadership, a new strategy, a thorough restructuring and particularly in making some fresh appointments. (This was, in effect, a 'cunning plan', Blackadder.)

- Whilst there were a number of constraining forces, these were overall weaker than the enabling forces. Even these, Lord Thurso managed to eradicate or mitigate with his cunning change plan.

But, we always need to ask the question "What is the One Big Thing we have forgotten?" Probably it is the traditional culture of Champney's which was the missing constraining force from the 1998 picture we see in Figure 23.

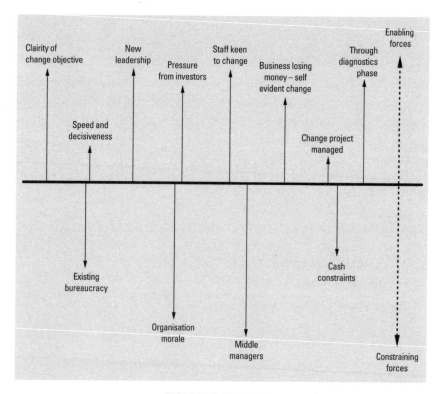

FIGURE 23: FORCE FIELD ANALYSIS AT CHAMPNEY'S

Lord Thurso's own larger-than-life character was a crucial ingredient in signalling that the changes necessary were very, very real, and also the need for *stretch* (Hamel). He reflects on the progress of his customer service project, which is also closely linked to the ongoing project of *culture change* (1997 interview):

> *"But the key at the top should have a kind of evangelical fanaticism about what the strategy is. Unless you have this, you are not going to manage to convince people. For example, last year I called our plans 'Going from Good-to-Great'. And we didn't go from Good-to-Great, we got better. So I said 'This is Good-to-Great' part two. We could be back here next year doing part three or even part four. But one day we will get there and I ain't leaving here until we do.*
>
> *I believe that all human beings are capable of change for the better. This may be an optimistic view. But I therefore start from the premise that it is better to work with people rather than change them. I find that the grass on the other side of the fence is not often greener. (Echoing Kanter and Peters.)*
>
> *When you are sorting out a business and getting the headcount right, yes you have to cut to get it right. But some people would go in and say, 'I can't work with that General Manager' and fire them and get another one. And then after six months you get another one. Personally I prefer to say 'Why is this not working? Let us look at it and actually help this person.' I find that you then get staff who are more loyal."*

But this involves recognising that staff's agendas (Piercy) may not be nicely aligned with the vision. Lord Thurso tells us about the practicalities of achieving the necessary culture change – another breakthrough strategy – to radically shift old behaviour patterns (1997 interview), indicating that change of this kind can take a long time (Johnson and Scholes, Welch):

> *"If I am honest with you I am only a small part the way through. All the things, these wonderful things that managers do, that is all part of our game. But the guy at the bottom says 'Sod you, I only have forty hours to do my job'. What he is saying to you is 'if you want me to do this, give me a reason'.*

And that guy at the bottom isn't going to say, 'Wow, that guy at the top he is a 'zing', now I will suddenly smile at customers'. There has got to be something in it for him. And part of it is being controlled, led, cajoled, pushed into it. And a part of it is being rewarded, feeling nice, all of the rest of it. It is a huge culture change that virtually every company in this country needs to actually genuinely understand what a customer-orientated organisation is. I have grave difficulty in thinking of a truly customer-orientated organisation in the United Kingdom. I mean, there must be one somewhere.

You do have to have a strategy. You can fight battles without a strategy and have success but it is a pretty haphazard thing. You have got to have a clear idea of where you are going, but equally you have to recognise that the achievement of the strategy will be a series of tactical steps." (Mintzberg's deliberate strategy, Sun Tzu – fighting battles.)

It is also necessary to look at how implementation difficulty changes over time. Initially, Lord Thurso's turnaround project faced severe difficulties. But once the new structure was put in place, and once Lord Thurso's new *vision* for the organisation had been unveiled, this difficulty would be mitigated.

As time progressed this difficulty increased at certain times as the organisation found a new stability and sought to resist further changes. In turn this difficulty was then reduced once Lord Thurso's programmes to improve customer service and to shift attitudes began to bite.

Looking now at the key *stakeholders* (Piercy), who had an influence on this strategic change, we see that:

- before Lord Thurso unveiled his turnaround strategy the balance of influence in the organisation was against him (especially the existing middle and senior managers).

- but by introducing new stakeholders (including two new senior managers), exiting some old ones, and by appealing directly to the staff, the balance of influence was reversed – in Lord Thurso's favour (see Figure 24).

Figure 24 is an impressive turnaround in the balance of power within the organisation – again down to Lord Thurso's cunning plan.

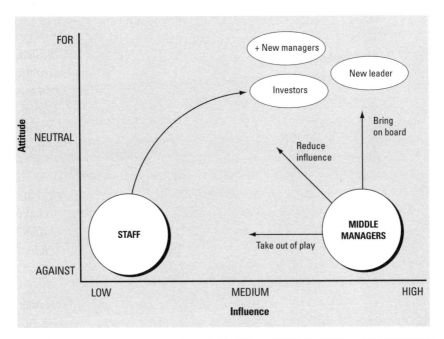

FIGURE 24: CHAMPNEY'S STAKEHOLDER ANALYSIS

To understand the influence patterns of these *stakeholders* (Piercy, Grundy and Brown – 'Be Your Own Strategy Consultant') we must also bear in mind some additional factors:

- The agendas of stakeholders are not fixed but will change over time vis-a-vis the various projects as new issues arise and as perceptions change within the organisation (Grundy).

- At any point in time agendas may be fluid and ambiguous, particularly at the start of the turnaround. Key stakeholders, particularly middle managers, may not have any clear attitude at all. Although they may have some core agendas (such as "I want to hang onto my job") these might be very limited. And even here, core agendas might be conditional on Champney's being seen as a congenial atmosphere to work in, given its new leadership. Never assume therefore that attitudes and underlying agendas of stakeholders are always givens.

- Individuals within one group will influence the agendas of others within the group. Through the informal network opinion leaders will signal their approval or disapproval of particular actions (as a *system* – Senge).

- You may need to break down the strategy into a number of sub-strategies – as stakeholder positions will vary according to what is being implemented (Grundy). For instance, a stakeholder may approve of Lord Thurso's plans to renovate the buildings, also approve of his plans to end the 'Health-For-Life' promotion, but be violently against running a smaller department.

We will now summarise Champney's strategic breakthroughs (Johnson and Scholes), which then provided the vehicle for turning strategic thinking into reality (Grundy – 'Strategic Project Management').

A summary of Champney's strategic change breakthroughs

Champney's strategic change projects according to the categories of 'strategic', 'operational' and 'organisational' are as follows:

- Strategic programmes – for a new business strategy (Ansoff, Hamel and Prahalad).

- Marketing strategy – involving market research and brand strategy.

- Business case.

- Exit time-sharing.

- Operational and systems projects – for an effective resource base (Grant).

- Sampling of services.

- Customer service improvement.

- Premises upgrade.

- Management process simplification.

- Management reporting.
- Customer database enhancement.
- Organisational projects – for a responsive organisation (Ulrich and Lake).
- Management re-structuring.
- Management recruitment.
- Maintaining staff morale.
- Culture change.
- Communication plan.
- Organisational skills diagnosis.

Later on we expand on the first bullet point above, strategic programmes, by examining some options for Champney's competitive strategy (Porter) which have been thought about in the past.

Not only do the above strategic breakthroughs gain in attractiveness through being part of a set of aligned and mutually supportive programmes, but they also gain through reduced implementation difficulty.

Key lessons from the Champney's case

In summary, the key lessons for using strategic thinking (Mintzberg) through the strategic change process (Johnson and Scholes) and especially those that impact on people and behaviour specifically are:

- Stakeholder analysis (Piercy): is absolutely central to managing the various strategic breakthroughs effectively. Accordingly, sufficient strategic thinking time should be devoted to analysing the current and potentially future positions of stakeholders – and their driving agendas.
- Leadership (Pascale, Peters Kanter): is crucial in a situation where stakeholders are likely to actively resist implementation efforts. This leadership requires a degree of evangelical enthusiasm, a great

practical tenacity in implementing that vision, and a continual openness to the environment of strategic change through strategic thinking.

- Achieving headway depends on building a sufficient 'stakeholder platform' (Piercy) to leverage off. This involved (at Champney's) key appointments of a new Finance Director and Property Manager – and winning over Champney's front-line staff.

- The difficulty over time of a strategic change or particular strategic project will vary over time (Grundy and Brown, 'Strategic Project Management'). The shifts in difficulty need to be anticipated and managed rather than just coped with, which requires strategic thinking to sense the future.

- There are invariably more options which can be addressed through strategic thinking than most managers normally think about (Ohmae).

Champney's – Some options for competitive strategy

A considerable range of options have come up over the years for what Champney's might have done (or might still do) based on 'strategy as stretch' and 'competing for the future' (Hamel and Prahalad). These include:

- Market sectors:
  - the corporate market – the younger market
  - professionals, generally
  - the 'mass' market (but not necessarily down-market).

- Geography (see Bartlett and Ghoshal, Yip):
  - the US tourist market
  - middle-Eastern market – continental Europe
  - via franchise (on cruise liners).

- Customers:
  - the 'pamper yourself' customer
  - the stressed-out person
  - the exploratory, alternative treatments type
  - the health fanatic
  - men (in their own right).
- Value creation (see Rappaport, Grundy):
  - more focus on guiding customers through treatments
  - after-care – between visits, as part of a continual 'better life' process, e.g. through help-line, home visits
  - more focus on stress and life style.
- Change of use to, for example (Ansoff):
  - a management centre
  - an up-market retreat
  - therapy for worn out, rich people, including pop stars, football stars
  - weekend dating activities.
- Value creating activities (Grundy, Slyvosky):
  - franchising
  - smaller Champney's centres (actually now implemented).
- Alliances (Lorange and Roos):
  - with a food company (to market Champney's brand)
  - with a restaurant company (who might deliver food to Champney's recipes)
  - with a cruise line or other up-market leisure providers.
- Acquisitions (Haspeslagh and Jemison):
  - to acquire and develop a second site, with a different catchment area (for example, in the North of England or in Scotland).

- Divest or outsource (Campbell et al):
    - perhaps to sell some of Champney's land, as a highly exclusive set of flats
    - to sell Champney's to another buyer (Haspeslagh and Jemison), either:
        - as soon as possible
        - after the business was turned around, or
        - on the back of the rise in property prices in 1998-2000.
- To float all or part of the business (McTaggart et al).

Interestingly, the most common options most people come up with are 'to make Champney's more exclusive and to re-market it to its core market', which is actually the option which Lord Thurso adopted.

Most groups who work on this case study underestimate the cost of this strategy (Champney's invested around £6.75 million) and fail to think through the possibilities for Champney's coming under greater competitive pressure (Porter). Also, Champney's traditional positioning might (some day) be not quite in fitting with customer demand.

Occasionally groups do come up with the 'sell the business' or *divestment* option, reflecting in part the tendency to hang onto what you have already got, rather than thinking who might be the best corporate parent for a particular business (Campbell et al).

Some lines of enquiry possibly open up then peter out. For instance, Lord Thurso reflects (2000 interview) on diversification (Ansoff):

> *"For example, we looked at opening restaurants. Now I am not saying that we won't open restaurants, but I have put it to one side for a while. We happen to produce stunningly good food.*
>
> *I have had conversations with a supermarket chain but at the end of the day... if you go to Birds Eye, for example, or Nestle... they very quickly say 'Actually, we can invent a brand and in the short-term your name, Champney's, won't help us'. It is an area which remains of interest to me."*

The range of options which can be generated for Champney's underlines the need to think much broader about 'options' through strategic thinking, than is conventionally done (Grundy).

Each of these options can then be mixed with others through a mix-and-match process, for example Champney's could hold alternative treatment sessions at one-day sessions for professional, stressed-out people (with their partners), delivered through an alliance (Lorange and Roos) with an up-market hotel group.

Organisational strategy – Options

When doing the exercise on *organisational* (or HR) *strategy* (Ulrich, Grundy) no one has ever wanted to keep the organisation much as it was. Invariably, managers go for at least halving current numbers, and some take it down as far as six or even less.

Whilst Champney's delivers very high levels of service in comparison with other organisations, its value-creating activities are (Porter's value chain, Grundy's using value system), if broken down, not unduly complex. Further, apart from IT there is little technology base (currently) to manage and develop.

The main roles which are often identified are:

- A Managing Director: to provide leadership, strategic thinking and challenge.
- A General Manager: to deliver day-to-day excellent service.
- A Financial and Commercial Director.
- A Marketing and Sales Manager (perhaps reporting to the Financial and Commercial Director).
- An HR Manager.

Breaking this down into sub-options:

- The Finance Director might have been supplied for the first nine months on a loan basis – to help sort Champney's out. After that a Financial Manager could suffice, once Champney's became steady-state.

- The HR Manager's role might be part-time, subsumed into that of the General Manager – supported with some outside HR consultancy.

It would be crucial that the Financial and Commercial Director or the Marketing and Sales Manager had the *competencies* (Hamel and Prahalad) to develop the sales database.

Here we see conventional structure thus semi-dissolving with a number of leaders managing fluid, strategic projects rather than making the assumption that for every value-creating activity there must be a role, there must therefore be an incremental person, and therefore there must be a cost. (This invites a Handy-esque view of the ideal organisation.)

Following the Champney's case study, the following is a useful exercise.

EXERCISE
Reflections on the Champney's case

- What parallels are there (if any) between Champney's organisation and your own? (For example, in its strategic drift, its internal rigidities, and its focus on the internal environment over and above the outside world.)

- What parallels are there between Champney's strategic change process (Johnson and Scholes) and the way change is managed in your own business (Kanter, Pascale, Peters), especially in the extent to which strategic thinking guides the change, or perhaps does not?

Case postscript

In August 2002 (and after Lord Thursoe had left the business to become a full-time politician in 2001), Champney's was sold to the Henlow Grange Leisure Group which owns two other health farms in the UK and was seeking to develop overseas.

Commentators at the time were somewhat surprised by that:

1   because Champney's was much more up-market than the Henlow Group;

2   it had (arguably) a much higher standard of leadership and of customer service;

3   there appeared little that Henlow could bring to Champney's – either in the way of its core competencies, accelerating market development, or through cost synergies.

Conclusion

The Champney's case study gives us a fascinating real-time account of how strategic thinking (Mintzberg) can be used to guide strategic change (Johnson and Scholes). It also highlights that there may be many *options* which can be created – even in an apparently tightly constrained situation, and thus there can be many *strategic degrees of freedom* (Ohmae). These options can then be manipulated by 'mix and match' to evolve even better, and potentially cunning, strategies.

The case study also highlighted the equal importance of thinking through cunning options for implementation (Blackadder).

Finally, Champney's underlined the need to create a joint sense of personal and business need to do strategic thinking. Lord Thurso's final reflection is (2000 interview):

"There are very, very few people who just do that with no pressure at all [think strategically]. If you are comfortable, well paid, good job, and good prospects on the horizon, when the company's making money, unless someone says growth is necessary then you won't think about it."

Summary of key points

The key points from this case study include:

- Strategic change often demands a complex set of external and internal breakthroughs – all of which need to be skilfully prioritised (Grundy).

- Whilst there were a considerable number of strategic options (Johnson and Scholes) for Champney's, it was probably even more important to apply strategic thinking to the implementation process than it was to identify the 'perfect strategy' (assuming of course that such a thing actually exists).

- Organisational structure issues are perhaps best addressed through the 'Spice Girl' approach of determining 'what do we really, really want?' (Ulrich and Lake).

- It is imperative to have an overarching vision to guide strategic thinking about the implementation process (Hamel and Prahalad).

- Strategic thinking needs to focus very much on finding the optimal communication plan (and style) for the strategy (Pascale, Peters).

- Potentially, Champney's could have gone for a wider set of strategic options: usually there are many possibilities which need to be stored up as latent strategies – for the future (Johnson and Scholes, Hamel and Prahalad).

- Stakeholder agendas (Piercy) need skilful diagnosis through strategic thinking.

FIVE
Marks & Spencer and the business strategy gurus

Introduction

This case study on Marks & Spencer presents some considerable management challenges. When a company as successful as Marks & Spencer appears to lose its way then it is far from obvious as to the most appropriate strategy which it should adopt (Johnson and Scholes). It is all too easy to try to manage incrementally within the current mindset (Quinn). Alternatively, in desperation sometimes strategies may be adopted which – although innovative – merely plunge the company into even deeper crisis, becoming *unrealised* ('strategic drift' Mintzberg) or *submergent* (Grundy).

This case study illustrates:

- Acquisitions
- Alliances
- Bargaining position
- Bureaucracy
- Competencies
- Competitive advantage
- Competitive positioning
- Competitive strategy
- Competitive rivalry
- Contention

- Corporate strategy
- Core competence
- Cost drivers
- Culture
- Deliberate strategy
- Demergers
- Differentiation
- Diversification
- Divestment
- Dominance

- Economic profit
- Emergency strategy
- Emergent strategy
- Entrants
- Financial strategy
- Focus strategy
- Gap analysis
- Global strategy
- HR strategy
- Legacy
- Logical incrementalism
- Paradigms
- Options
- Resource-based competitive advantage
- Scenarios

- Supplier base
- Shareholder value
- Strategic change
- Strategic fit
- Strategic leadership
- Substitutes
- Sustainability
- Vision
- Uncertainty
- HR strategy
- Legacy
- Logical incrementalism
- Paradigms
- Options

The main case study is set out as follows:

- Marks & Spencer – its position mid-1990s.
- Marks & Spencer – its position 1997-2001.
- Future options for Marks & Spencer.

Marks & Spencer – The position mid-1990s

In 1994 Marks & Spencer PLC was a very large, successful business with a turnover of £6.5 billion and profits before tax of £851 million. Fourteen million customers then shopped at M&S each week.

M&S must have been exposed to many opportunities over the past ten to twenty years which would have been strategic temptation but had, by and large, chosen to build on its core business and capability (Hamel and Prahalad).

Where M&S had come unstuck – in parts of its *global* development (Bartlett and Ghoshal, Yip) and in *acquisition* (Haspeslagh and Jemison) – is where it had stepped outside its (then) core capability (Ansoff, Ulrich and Lake). But these setbacks may well have prevented M&S from fully capitalising on other avenues for strategic development, nearer to home, for example, into other service industries in the UK and elsewhere.

M&S's core business focused on high street retailing, and core products are clothing for all the family – women's, men's and children's. This 'general' business contributed nearly £3.8 billion of turnover. In 1994 it had also built a very successful niche food business which now amounted to a surprising £2.6 billion of turnover (40 per cent of the group). In the 1990s M&S had successfully *diversified* (Ansoff) into personal financial services (although this business is still relatively small compared with the core). Growth has been primarily of an organic nature and overseas ventures (acquisitive and organic) have met with variable success. The most successful ventures appear to have been organic and have involved *alliances* with local companies from whom M&S has been able to learn (Lorange and Roos).

M&S's gross profit divided by turnover (or 'gross margin') had increased from 32.8 per cent in 1990 to 35.1 per cent in 1994 – with no decreases year-on-year during the severe UK recession in the early 1990s. This was a truly impressive achievement and represented a very hard act to follow. How could M&S sustain this stretching performance into the late 1990s? This was to present a huge challenge.

M&S's annual report and accounts did not, unfortunately, give a breakdown of operating profit by type of trading activity – indeed M&S is not (legally) obliged to. However, it is safe to conjecture that the 20 per cent of business activities (by number of activities) which have formed over 80 per cent of profit generation are (as an approximation):

- men's and women's clothing;
- the food business.

This left home furnishings, children's wear, men and women's shoes, financial services and other products as generating probably around 20 per cent of profit. Also over 80 (in fact 87) per cent of activities were then located in a single country – the UK. Increasingly, M&S was beginning to source from non-UK suppliers, having overcome its earlier hesitation.

A summary table of M&S results is shown in Figure 25. This shows a remarkable stability in the mix of corporate business over a four-year period.

Its first half interim results for the 1994 year end highlighted relatively sluggish growth in food sales (at 3.9 per cent) relative to general business (posting an impressive 8.9 per cent growth). This highlighted perhaps the tougher competitive constraints impacting on its UK food business. It also highlighted why M&S might be tempted into a major push for growth outside the UK.

If we go back even further in time (to 1985), M&S had achieved a compound rate of growth in turnover of around 8 per cent in nominal terms over nine years. On the other hand, during much of that period we saw fairly high annual doses of inflation, particularly in the overheated late 1980s and into the earlier part of the recession in the UK. So what was perhaps more impressive was M&S's stability and consistency of development rather than its percentage real growth per se.

	1994		1992		1990	
Turnover	£m		£m		£m	
General	3786	58%	3371	58%	3221	58%
Foods	2632	40%	2358	40%	2306	41%
Financial activities	123	2%	98	2%	81	1%
	6541	100%	5827	100%	5608	100%
Operating profit	873	13.3% of sales	635	10.9% of sales	305	5.4% of sales
Earnings per share	20.9p		13.5p		6.9p	

FIGURE 25: A BRIEF SUMMARY OF M&S FINANCIAL PERFORMANCE 1994-1990
(Source: M&S Annual Report and Accounts, March 1994).

The main driver of increased *economic profit* (Rappaport) over 1985 to 1994 was the improvement in operating margin, up from 9.4 per cent of turnover to 13.0 per cent. This kind of improvement could come in a number of forms – higher prices, fewer or lower discounts, or supplier productivity improvements/M&S holding supplier prices down, and delaying refurbishments. Much of that improvement came through M&S exercising its very strong *bargaining position* vis-à-vis suppliers. But if that were to be the case, then did M&S have much further scope to squeeze suppliers or otherwise improve margins? Did it need to seek other avenues for development to sustain its earnings growth? These were questions raised perhaps prophetically by commentators at the time (Grundy, 1994).

Marks & Spencer – Recipes for success

M&S's success depended upon a philosophy of value for money, quality and service. It had built an extremely strong brand which had an appeal to a high proportion of the 'middle market' in the UK who had high brand loyalty. (To illustrate, M&S claimed to have 35 per cent of the British market for bras and knickers, thus being *dominant*.)

M&S was very selective in having quality locations and relatively simple product ranges (thus having a *'focus strategy'* Porter). It was also selective in the things which it did not do – for example, it did not (then) take other's people's credit cards and avoided high fashion, etc. It was also (justifiably) famed for insisting in the absolute best from its suppliers – a distinctive *competence* (Hamel and Prahalad), and also part of its *resource-based competitive advantage*. According to one City of London investment analyst (on Channel 4):

> "Being a supplier to Marks & Spencer is a source of unprecedented pressure, and some might say is interference from a customer in those businesses. If you are producing markets which are good enough to Marks, at a price which is acceptable to Marks, and the other conditions of being a Marks & Spencer supplier are satisfied, then being a supplier to Marks & Spencer is very, very profitable."

In the mid-1980s M&S began to lose ground to new competitors, such as Next, which targeted M&S and offered quality clothes with just that bit more fashion *increasing rivalry* (Porter). This attack was good for M&S, which for a period regained much of the initiative.

M&S had also had a variable track record overseas and had had a number of disappointments both in North America (for instance in Canada where M&S traded for 22 years, according to the *Financial Times*, 1994) and in Europe. Like many companies which have developed a very strong market penetration of a single national country, M&S had found it hard to adapt its strategic and growth recipes to quite new and different business environments (Yip). For example, in Spain, it was said that while local people liked M&S underwear, etc, they found the original clothes offered 'ugly' (*Financial Times*, 1994). This invited the question as to whether M&S's merchandising in Spain was originally driven by a tailoring of the UK offering, rather than by working backwards from local tastes reflecting inappropriate deployment of competency (Grant, Ulrich and Lake).

Whatever one thinks of this *global* development strategy, there is no doubt that M&S was seeking to exploit those opportunities in a big, albeit still somewhat cautious way.

According to an investment analyst in the City of London (Channel 4):

> "I think a much bigger proportion of its profits will come from conti-nental Europe over the next 10, 15, 20 years. There is room for growth in France, maybe into Germany. But I also think that there are very exciting prospects in the Far East. It is already well established in Hong Kong and of course the great unknown is whether it might get into China."

In fact M&S intended to double its selling space in continental Europe over the 1994-1997 period, with Germany and Italy (in addition to France and Spain) on the agenda. (The first German stores were announced in March 1995 – *Financial Times*, 28 March).

According to Sir Richard Greenbury, then Chairman, who appeared to get carried away by 'globalisation' (Yip):

"There isn't a retailer, a big one, in the world today that can probably say that he is going to stay in his home-based economy, and just do well there. I mean all the great retailers are having to face the facts that they have yet to take their skills abroad, one way or another." (Channel 4.)

Perhaps M&S was now much better placed to understand how to exploit its talents internationally than during its earlier experimental efforts. Maybe by recruiting more staff of other nationalities (especially in senior roles) would have helped, so as to adapt the M&S philosophy to other environments. This may seem to be a minor issue at first sight but could, in the longer term, be major as it shapes the mindset of management.

M&S's *competitive advantage* in 1994 (Ohmae, Porter, Grant) was based (in order of *ease of imitation*, beginning with the most difficult things to imitate first) on:

- M&S brand.
- Value-for-money (as of 1994).
- Very high market share in niche markets (e.g. luxury food and women's underwear).
- Supplier linkages and innovation.
- Systems.
- Sites.

M&S's brand was then supported by a reputation for value for money and also by its reputation for customer service (and its supporting *culture*). Around these core *competencies* were clustered M&S's supplier linkages and innovation which were also *core sources of competitive advantage* (Grant). According to one City of London investment analyst (Channel 4):

"Marks has styled itself the manufacturer without factories... They probably do have the closest relationship with suppliers of any UK retailer."

Whilst this list of (then) competitive advantages was impressive, these were potentially ones which could evaporate quickly especially vis a vis nimbler opposition (Stalk). One analyst reflected on this:

"I think they are a very self-confident company, and provided that they remain self-confident and not complacent I don't think that that's a problem. But I think that retailing is a notoriously fickle business. You have to keep on reinventing it and reinventing it year after year, season after season. You have to make sure that your clothes are fashionable, that the styles and colour are what people actually want." (Channel 4)

Some felt that (even then) M&S had become too rigid as an organisation (indeed in Mintzberg's organisational forms, a *bureaucracy*. Sir Richard Greenbury, chairman, espoused the dilemmas of maintaining discipline versus encouraging individual spontaneity:

"You must have discipline. You can't have everybody doing their own thing. And big businesses do become bureaucratic and they do become inflexible. But the day that they become so bureaucratic and inflexible that the free thinker, the maverick, the entrepreneur, the fellow or the woman who doesn't do it the conventional way ... those people must be given an opportunity to express their talents."

But did he really mean it? According to one (brave) joiner from another retailer (a department store) who took another view:

"People just don't say anything. No one will speak against the Chair, because they say it shouldn't be done. You can just see people's faces changing (when you say critical things). People just don't believe you, when you say something bad about Marks & Spencer, so you just don't bother." (Channel 4)

M&S also had some critical areas of competitive disadvantage as follows:

- M&S perhaps had an over-cautious approach to managing its strategic development (at least in terms of organic development in the UK – except for financial services), and its culture generally;

- Its apparent lack of flexibility (for example in refusing to take non-M&S credit or debit cards (until very recently – perhaps too much deliberate and not enough emergent strategy (Mintzberg)));

- Its UK-centred mind-set. This did not particularly affect its UK business but may have hampered its international development (Bartlett and Ghoshal), perhaps seriously.

As regards organisational rigidity, let us note the comments of another analyst (Channel 4):

"They [M&S] will certainly tend to be dismissive of criticism from outside. When you think about it, when a company is incredibly successful and Marks & Spencer has been, and still is, then your starting base has got to be, that what anyone outside is saying is potentially wrong, and that they know the best way to do things. They have been doing it like that for 20, 30, 40, 50 years and it works for them." (Its 'paradigm' (Johnson and Scholes) did seem to have been frozen in the past.)

One of the most distinctive elements of this culture was the attention to microscopic detail at most senior levels. On the UK Channel 4 television programme, Sir Richard Greenbury, chairman, interjected at the start of a meeting to discuss current M&S foods to point out that:

"I had the potato and leek [soup] last night and it has got lots of cream in it and it has got no potato in it. You know, if you have potato and leek then I like it to have a sort of powerful taste and it was, it was rich, it was too liquid, it just didn't gel with me."

This management *style* felt very much more like Braybrooke and Lindblom's *'muddling through'* rather than anything visionary like Kantnar, Peters or Pascale, and certainly not a *'learning organisation'* (Senge).

As a result of this input in a later scene the food group merchandisers were seen taking notes of his comments as if they were about to change the formula.

Yes, this intervention was an example of M&S's great strength ('Retail is Detail'). But how could this level of detailed intervention be possible in the future if M&S were ever successful in generating up to a quarter, a half, or even more sales outside the UK? Could M&S truly become a substantial and successful international retailer with this apparently high degree of centralised, top-down direction and control in its merchandising? (Bartlet and Ghoshal.)

Also, the issue of M&S's (then) *deliberate strategy* (Mintzberg) to refuse to take other credit or debit cards might have been seen as justified in terms of the virtue of strategic choice – saying no to a costly strategy with such a *cost driver* (Rappaport). However, the costs of excluding (or reducing) the business of many customers lacking M&S charge cards were considerable, if unquantified. Some customers maybe either have found it difficult or possibly too inconvenient to acquire M&S cards (for example, tourists).

Again, the history of M&S's attitude to non-M&S cards was symptomatic of a twin competitive strength and weakness. As one analyst (Channel 4) put it:

> *"You are looking at a company which essentially you have to charac-
> terise as a 'family dynasty', everyone is schooled in the history and in
> the traditions. I think the disadvantage of this kind of culture is that it
> can make it inward looking, it can perhaps breed a kind of arrogance."*
> Hinting that it would it very, very difficult to implement value migra-
> tion (Slyvosky).

Turning to M&S's global business, although M&S's brand strength had power and although M&S still had a clear market and product focus, it did not necessarily have complete fit with local cultures (or at least did not originally, as the various examples quoted earlier illustrated). Also, although M&S still had a strong supplier base this was offset by significant difficulties of logistics and attendant higher costs internationally. It was only in the late 1990s that M&S had been able to lift European sales. This success was achieved by exporting its 'outstanding value campaign' from the UK, and thus by reducing its prices and its margins significantly.

Marks & Spencer – The position 1997 – 2001

For most companies, competitive advantage needs to come from a number of sources and not just one. It is often the specific combination of competitive advantages that makes a company distinctive and which leads to superior performance (Hamel and Prahalad, Ohmae).

The main ingredients of competitive advantage that lead to superior performance are:

- customer value; or

- lower cost; or

- greater speed, flexibility or responsiveness than our competitors.

This can be made more concrete by defining specific criteria:

- **Value** – brand and reputation, market share, unique underlying skills and management skills.

- **Cost** – cost base, market share.

- **Speed** – distribution, unique operational skills and management skills (Stalk).

M&S's traditional brand strength was supported by the M&S reputation for value for money and also its reputation for customer service (and its supporting culture). M&S's supplier linkages and product innovation were also its traditional sources of *competitive advantage* (Grant).

From the previous section, M&S had an impressively strong bundle of multiple and reinforcing sources of *competitive advantage* during the period of 1990-1996, but it had become somewhat bureaucratic and rigid, and not particularly receptive to change (Peters, Porter).

By around 1997, M&S's business portfolio was of varying competitive strength (for instance, between clothing, food, other items and financial services, UK and internationally). Although M&S had some impressive product lines, particularly women's lingerie and its niche foods business, this was offset by a number of strategically and (probably) financially less interesting business areas.

The *diversified* area of financial services (Ansoff) also represented a potentially attractive opportunity to M&S. The particular strengths which M&S brought to this arena were its:

- brand awareness (if tarnished in recent times);
- reputation for quality and, at the same time, value for money; and
- focus on a narrower product line.

M&S did not, around 1997, change its strategic direction fundamentally other than to change the design focus of its clothes in an attempt to become more fashionable.

During the period 1997-1999 a number of external market shifts crystallised (Ansoff's weak signals):

1 Despite continued economic recovery, consumers became more discerning. Where they were asked to pay a premium, they appeared to want a brand and that brand was (at least in the young and middle-age groups) not M&S.

2 Because of an increase in the sales of *substitute items* (Porter) including mobile telephones, computers (including access to the Internet) and in overseas holidays (through cheap flights), a squeeze was put on the retail sector generally. M&S proved to be not well placed to withstand this.

3 *Competitive rivalry* for upmarket foods increased significantly, for example, by Tesco's 'Finest' lines, imitating M&S's differentiation/focus strategy (Porter).

4 M&S's *global expansion* (perhaps predictably) faltered, with a U-turn on investment in territories such as Germany.

5 New *entrants* to the UK retail market, like Gap and Matalan, (Porter) began to take more share of the younger market, pushing M&S up the age range where it was under increasing attack from Next and Debenhams.

6 The fashion cycle was accelerating so that the two-seasons-a-year merchandising process at M&S became unwieldy and obsolescent (Stalk).

Meanwhile, M&S continued to pursue its *global expansion* plans whilst its UK position came under increasing attack. This was reflected in M&S's more recent results, as set out in Figure 26:

Turnover	2002 £ million	2000 £ million	1999 £ million	1998 £ million	1997 £ million
General	4364	4629	4765	4811	4602
Foods	3420	3201	3110	3157	3024
Financial services	351	365	350	275	216
	8135	8195	8225	8243	7842
Operating profits	644	471	512	1103	1022
Earnings per share (per FRS 14)	5.4p	9.6p	13.0p	28.8p	26.2p

FIGURE 26: M&S FINANCIAL PERFORMANCE 1997-2002
(From Annual Report and Accounts, 2002)

M&S did make some major changes to its strategy in the period 1998-2000, as follows:

- It decided to partially abandon its dependency on its traditional brand, St Michael. Ambitious plans to develop more exciting merchandising ideas came from its 'Autograph' range. Trialled in its more prestigious stores, the plan was to get well known designers to design expensive, up-market clothes to be sold in a separately demarcated section of M&S. (This strategy met with only partial success, and by 2001 signals were given that M&S was to rethink this strategy.)

- Its previous chairman, Sir Richard Greenbury, eventually retired from the board. Sir Richard had overseen M&S's success in the early-mid 1990s, but now admitted (*Money Programme*, 2000) that its financial success was at least partially due to cost-cutting (Porter). With hindsight it was admitted that, given the investment in greater service by players like Tesco, this strategy might have been unwise. (Apparently the negative effects of this lower service strategy were not apparent to Sir Richard as stores would field all their part-timers on the days of his visits. He claimed not to have been aware of this practice.) Following considerable boardroom acrimony (beyond *contention*) of the like that even Peters and Pascale could hardly have envisaged), Sir Richard was replaced by a successful retailer, Luc Vandevelde, who stated his aim was to turn around M&S within two years. M&S's advertising campaign (on TV and on billboards) featured a 'normal sized', but attractive, lady taking her clothes off to celebrate her size 14 body – aiming to appeal to Ms and Mrs Average UK. Unfortunately, Ms and Mrs Average UK did not want to identify with that image, so the campaign backfired.

- M&S tried to enliven its underwear with *alliances* with Agent Provocateur appearing to push very aggressively into more adventurous and sensual markets. This again proved unsuccessful, and the M&S standalone lingerie shop pilot was halted. (Perhaps this venture was an over-reaction to highly visible criticisms of M&S's 'boring bras' – which we see later!)

- M&S recruited George Davies (ex Next) to form an *alliance* to create a new sub-brand, called Per Una. By May 2001 George Davies was reported to be having problems in timely sourcing for the new range.

By 1999, M&S's dividend per share was *only just* covered by current earnings, whereas in previous years it was twice covered by earnings.

In 2000, its profits after tax and after exceptional items were £258.7 million compared with a £258.6 million dividend, leaving a surplus of just £0.1 million.

At one shareholders' meeting one angry shareholder and customer brandished an M&S bra, claiming that it was so fundamentally unexciting that it was no wonder that customers were alienated an apparent lack of *strategic fit* caused by *strategic drift*.

Whilst M&S still has an enviably well-known brand and a deep customer loyalty in some *market segments*, there is no question that its brand had been significantly tarnished by internal events, by its market failures and by adverse commentary from many sources.

The half-year results to September 1999 revealed that M&S had made a number of changes, aimed at influencing both internal and external performance drivers:

1 **In management** – its long-standing chairman left the board and a number of other top-level management changes were made. (This was not a period which could easily be characterised as one of *strategic leadership*.) A number of television documentaries around the time suggested that Sir Richard had been somewhat autocratic – based on sources inside M&S. Whilst this style suited the 1992-1995 recessionary period it appeared not to be fruitful during 1996-1999, when M&S needed to become faster, more flexible and refocused. His exit followed a boardroom battle which involved Keith Oates, then a senior director, making a pre-emptive strike for the chief executive's role whilst Sir Richard was away on holiday. Keith Oates also then resigned. A marketing director was appointed (for the first time) and was recruited from outside.

2 **In its supplier base** – M&S moved fast to cut the less effective parts of its UK supplier base. Whilst this helped to reduce costs this also produced further bad publicity as thousands of manufacturing staff (not employed by M&S) lost their jobs. (Unfortunately, not all of these savings were to help M&S's bottom line, as they were needed to substantially reduce prices.)

3 **In marketing and promotion** – M&S began to advertise more aggressively and to introduce more aggressive promotions.

4 **In its credit card policy** – M&S decided to allow stores to accept credit cards for the first time in its history. This was to occur by Spring 2000.

5 **Repositioning of the stores** – by offering better value for money and improved service, and by better display and presentation of merchandise.

By late 2000/early 2001, M&S appeared to be in ever deeper trouble suggesting an unrealised *deliberate turnaround strategy* (Mintzberg). According to the *Financial Times* (January 24, 2001), Christmas trading had been even worse and, in the 16 weeks to January, group sales were down 3.1 per cent (down 5.1 per cent on a comparable store basis). Clothing, footwear and gifts were down 9.3 per cent. On the plus side, there was an improvement of 2.9 per cent in food. The 25 new concept stores were only 4 per cent ahead, despite expenditure of £60 million on refitting.

Mr Vandevelde, Executive Chairman, had given himself two years to turn the store around but time appeared to be running out. Perhaps unfairly, one analyst, Tony Shirt of Credit Suisse First Boston said:

> *"You cannot really say that there is a strategy here at all... the only strategy seems to be not to completely muck it up, rather than to recover. Everything is being run very defensively."* (Grundy's 'emergency strategy'.)

In March 2001 M&S announced new steps to turn the company around through some *re-engineering* (Hammer and Champy), including:

- Job cuts of 4,400.
- Closure of many European stores (divestment).
- Closure of a small number of UK stores.
- Closure of the Direct catalogues business.
- Sale of half of its Manchester flagship store to Selfridges.
- A share buy-back when property sales had gone through, Brooks Brothers in the US, and Kings Supermarkets *(Times*, March 30, 2001) – attempting to manage M&S's shareholder value (Rappaport) *(financial strategy)*.

Its Chairman asked for a further *three* years to successfully turn around the business. This would be through a return to a back-to-basics policy of 'classically-stylish' clothes aimed at the 35+ age group customers (*Mail on Sunday*, April, 2001). Casual observation of M&S's actual customer base during lunchtimes in its Marble Arch store in June 2001 indicated that around ninety per cent of its customers were between 35 and 60.

In May 2001, there were demonstrations outside M&S's Marble Arch store against its cuts and against the closure of M&S's European outlets (which appeared not to have been handled particularly well in PR terms). 2001 profits showed another fall of £36 million (on 1999) and Luc Vandevelde said he did not know whether sales would grow in 2002 (*Guardian*, May 23, 2001). In 2001 there was a further re-structuring charge of £335 million. This represented the third consecutive year of declining profits.

In a television interview Mr Vandevelde said that M&S's strategic drift and decline – Johnson and Scholes – (before his arrival) had occurred over a five-year period and *it would take about five years to reverse*.

Some key statistics were:

*   Like-for-like sales – down by 2.6%.
*   Clothing and general merchandise – down by 6.3%.
*   Food sales – up by 2.6%.

Luc Vandevelde also announced that M&S's head office would move to a new headquarters in Paddington Basin in around two years time, helping a change in *culture*.

Interestingly a new bonus scheme (the first of its kind at M&S) was to be introduced, offering big pay-outs 'even if M&S's profits continued to plunge' (according to reports). Apparently this was to ensure that successful business areas would not be penalised for poor performance elsewhere in the group. This attracted major adverse Press commentary in May-June 2001.

Luc Vandevelde was (in 2001) still assembling his new management team, the last of the old guard having left. Roger Holmes, CEO designate (headhunted from Kingfisher in January 2001) was still finding his feet and was putting the final finishes to the new team. Press comment was concerned that this team lacked really experienced retailers with flair (*core competencies*).

Thus, M&S clearly still faced an enormous challenge to turn itself around, having tackled these changes increment-by-increment (Quinn).

Marks & Spencer – Turning to the future

Clearly, in June 2001 M&S still faced a massive challenge to turn itself around – even in a three-year timescale. The repeated failures to deal effectively with problems had undermined external confidence not only in the organisation but also in the leadership of its new Chairman. The scale of the turnaround task was highlighted in a bench-marking visit by a group of chartered accountants who visited M&S's high profile Oxford Street store in London, in January 2001, as part of a case study exercise (*customer bench-marking*). The chartered accountants found a number of areas of poor customer value (Bowman, Grundy):

- The store was a rabbit warren which, given M&S's poor signage, was hard to navigate around.

- Its 'look' appeared old-fashioned, and attempts to brighten it up with a couple of TV screens showing videos seemed to create an even worse, patchy effect.

- Merchandising was not well displayed, with piles of unsold clothes cluttering up the stores, presumably left over from the sale.

- With one or two exceptions (with more healthy convenience foods) M&S's food range appeared almost identical to that offered ten years ago. M&S foods seemed to have been stuck in a kind of time warp.

- There was a tiny office bar situated at the back of foods in the basement (not the best place to generate footfall). This was unattended – spaces were there for three clocks showing the times in London, Los Angeles and Singapore. The Singapore clock was missing and the Los Angeles clock time was wrong. What had happened to M&S's famed attention to detail and discipline? (*Core competence.*)

If aliens had visited this store (after being briefed on how successful M&S had been throughout 1975-1995) they would have had a real surprise – if not a shock. What had gone wrong?

Drawing the helicopter view out of this analysis, it would not have taken seven hundred pages of a strategy consultant's report (which was rumoured to have been presented to M&S top management in 2000) to have realised that:

"M&S strategy needs still to be fundamentally rethought."

and

"Incremental tinkering with that strategy is not going to work."

The scene was therefore set for M&S to conduct a more radical review of its strategic and financial options...

EXERCISE
Strategic options

Using the strategic option grid (Figure 4), what options could you see for Marks and Spencers (as at 2002), and how attractive are these options? What *scenarios* can you paint for their potential success or failure? (Do the scores please?)

Conclusion

The Marks and Spencer case study provides us with a graphic account of the relevance of the strategy gurus – in the context of strategic change. Where might M&S now be if it had performed the kind of 'Helicopter' analysis which we provided for you in the case study – and hopefully was also suggested by your own options, which might have resulted in an unbundling/rebirth of M&S's corporate portfolio?

SIX
Checklists for managing strategy

Introduction

In this short chapter we give you some useful supplementary checklists for managing your strategy as follows:

- Organic business development strategies.
- Strategic and financial planning generally.
- Restructuring strategies.
- Information systems strategies.
- Management buy-out strategies.
- Alliance and joint venture strategies.
- Operational strategies.

These checklists are useful for live business strategies and also for MBA coursework, and for MBA projects and dissertations.

Organic business development strategies

These checklists will help to flesh out some of the richer content issues which you may well come up against in evaluating projects. Whilst managers may feel they are well-versed in these organic development projects, they may well look too myopically at the more obvious areas of inquiry.

Organic business development projects can be aimed at a number of areas including:

1 New products.

2 New markets – by sector or by geography.

3 Selling more to existing customers.

4 New value-creating activities.

5 New distribution channels.

6 New technologies.

Let's now look at some core checklists for each of the areas outlined above.

New product strategies

It is often said that nine out of ten new product ideas fail either because they are not thought through sufficiently in themselves or (and more commonly) the product concept does not quite match market need. These checklists should help you get a better steer. Our questions now are:

- How fast is the market for this type of product growing?

- How much competitive pressure exists in its market?

- How well does the product meet its target customer needs; what are the turn-ons and turn-offs from a customer point of view?

- Which other products is it competing with and what are the relative advantages/disadvantages between each?

- How (if at all) does the product need servicing, and what are the relative competitive advantages here?

- How complex is the product, and will this level of complexity mean it is:
  - a) harder to launch,
  - b) less flexible to change subsequently?
- Are there any wonderfully innovative features (which add real value) to the product?
- If these exist, how easily can these be imitated?
- How consistent is the organisation's capability and mind-set with this product, and what implementation issues might this raise?
- What skills training is required to support this product effectively?
- Are the product's long-run unit costs likely to be sustainable longer-term?
- What other changes in the organisation (for example, to key business processes or to organisational structure) are needed?
- Will the sales force and distribution channels accommodate the new product effectively – without destruction, disruption, a dilution of sales of other products?
- To what extent might the product cannibalise on other existing products?
- To what extent will the product's innovation be project-managed well?
- How can its introduction be positioned and accelerated in the organisation?

New market strategies

New market development strategies may overlap to some extent with new products. Nevertheless, we include some new questions to supplement those on new products:

- Have you systematically prioritised which (of the potential new markets) it would be most attractive to address (for example, using the Strategic Option Grid)?

- How inherently attractive is this market (consider its growth drivers and the level of competitive pressure in it)?

- How difficult is it to operate within that market (generally)?

- Do we have the natural competencies to do well in that market?

- Is this market culturally vastly different to our current core markets?

- Is this a market especially prone to discounting, high costs of satis-fying customers or distribution channels, or low margins generally?

- Have we got a genuinely 'cunning' entry strategy (or just an average one)?

- What channel strategy options exist and which of these is

  a) most attractive inherently (in terms of its use and value-added generally),

  b) one where we have greatest competitive advantage?

- What are the most critical uncertainties about that market and how can we minimise our exposure to these?

- Will entering this particular market foreclose options to enter other markets?

- To what extent will market conditions vary internationally, and which of these markets should we really give highest priority?

Selling more to existing customers

Selling more to our existing customers may well be a neglected strategy but, nevertheless, one which might be both highly attractive and relatively easy:

- Which of our existing customer base could we potentially sell more to?

- What could we sell them, why and how?

- What things have prevented us from selling as much as our true potential to existing customers in the past?

- What latent, existing needs could we satisfy, which we are not currently satisfying?

- What latent, future needs could we satisfy, and how?

- How might selling more to our existing customers strengthen our relationship with them and gain lock-in?

- Are there other buyers within the customer's organisation which we can sell to (e.g. another management function, another division, etc)?

- What specific sales or other incentives would encourage greater penetration of our existing customer base?

- Which of our key competitors is currently active with these customers and how can we erode their share?

- How can we make it unbelievably easy to buy from us (and to buy more from us)?

- How can these improvements be project managed?

New value-creating activities

Adding value in new ways may offer exciting strategic opportunities but ones which managers may find it difficult to think through:

- Are there new ways in which we can add value to the customer (value-creating activities)?

- How much additional value is likely to be created for them – from their perspective?

- How will we be able to capture or share this value creation given our relative bargaining power and our longer-term strategy?

- To what extent should new value-creating activities be in or out-sourced, and why?

- How readily might new ways of adding value be imitated by competitors?

- To what extent will customers seek to do these value-creating activities themselves (assuming they are worthwhile having)?

- What is our natural level of competence for adding value in these new ways?

- Can we easily pilot these new value-creating opportunities?

- How will we project manage developing these new value-creating activities?

New distribution channel strategies

Opening up new distribution channels avoids the difficulties of new product and/or market innovation – and may well be cheap. But in order to avoid diluting our strategy and shareholder value, we will need to be relatively selective:

- How much margin are we likely to obtain from a new distribution channel?

- How difficult is it likely to be to deal with?

- What are the key alternatives to dealing with this particular channel (for example by the Internet, sales force, an alliance, etc)?

- Will this particular channel lead to conflict with any other distribution channels and, if so, how will we manage it?

- Are we likely to get a high level of returns or other quality problems through this channel?

- Will the channel actually understand our product sufficiently well?

- How much support will this channel put behind our product – relative to that of other products?

- Does this distribution channel have something that fits our natural competencies and our culture?

- How competitive is this particular channel relative to other pathways to a market?

- If we do not use this channel, what (if anything) is the biggest downside?

- How would we project manage a new entry to that channel?

New technologies

New technologies may be a turn-on to middle managers but a turn-off to top managers (whose main focus is to extract short and medium-term values out of the business). We may therefore need some testing questions in order to screen innovative technology projects:

- Does the technology actually fit with our present or emerging definition of 'the business(es) we are in'?

- Do we really understand the technology?

- What other things (other than technology) all have to line up to deliver real value? (Use a 'Wishbone' analysis.)

- Are we doing the project mainly because of its sheer technological edge, and because it is inherently exciting – or because it will generate real value, and value that we can actually harvest?

- What key value and cost drivers are impacted on by the new technology?

- What new skills do we need to fully exploit any new technology?

- To what extent do we have to change our mind-set in order to get the very best out of the new technology?

- Where the technology relies heavily on the Internet, how easy is it for our business model to be copied or imitated?

- How quickly will the new technology spread and where there are customer turn-offs in its use, how can these be mitigated or removed?

- How rapidly might the technology be superseded by further technologies and how vulnerable does this therefore make our strategy?

- What substitute technologies are available which are in many respects better right now?

- How should we project manage the introduction of the new technology?

Strategic and financial planning processes

A strategic (and financial) plan is a complex activity which involves a number of outputs and a variety of stakeholders – with different involvement. This is an area for project management par excellence – and yet one which is only peripherally touched on by most strategy text books. It is also an area frequently managed not very well within organisations generally.

- Does the 'strategic' plan genuinely take into account the impact of external change?

- Does it involve the specific measurement of competitive advantage or disadvantage in terms of value added (and at what cost) to target customers vis-a-vis key competitors?

- Is it consistent with 'mission' and is this 'mission' credible given the risk and uncertainties in achieving strategic goals?

- Is financial appraisal used to evaluate the economic value of business strategies (i.e. in cash flow terms – and not just 'reported' earnings projections) or are these strategies left untested in terms of shareholder value?

- Is the strategy feasible given current financial constraints, and do these 'constraints' need testing themselves?

- Does the strategic plan reflect the organisational and operational capability (strengths and weaknesses) of the business – can we excel in what we propose?

- Are there clear strategic and financial milestones for success which link to quarterly or bi-annual business performance assessment?

- Is the 'strategic plan' communicated in appropriate detail to sufficient relevant levels of management and staff responsible for implementation?

- Is there adequate scope for 'emergent strategies' to develop within the overall strategic and financial framework (i.e. in-built provision for innovation and exploitation of hard-to-foresee opportunity)?

- Are adequate change project mechanisms set in place to implement the strategy? (For example, change project teams, off-site review workshops, rewards for actions to implement change, etc.)

Restructuring strategies

Restructuring strategies are now undertaken on an almost routine basis by most larger organisations. Restructuring is often managed in relative isolation from other projects and is also positioned as geared towards delivering more shorter-term benefits. Restructuring, if managed as a strategy, can be handled much more effectively than this, especially if the following questions are addressed:

- Is the rationale for the restructuring fully thought through and does this reflect not merely current needs but anticipate pending changes in the business?

- Is there a history of frequent re-structuring which has resulted in a permanent (and unnecessary) state of instability in the organisation? (If so, how can this be managed more strategically in the future?)

- Has the restructuring put managers into 'artificial' positions without genuine business benefits which are patently transparent and which will aggravate organisational ambiguity?

- Are new appointees genuinely capable of being effective in their roles given their skills, their style, and also the degree of teamworking within the organisation?

- Has the restructuring been communicated in such a way to lay bare the business-led reasons for the restructuring?

- What is the timing of announcement of restructuring – has it been deliberately timed so as to prevent reflection and debate and thereby result in simmering resentment?

- How does the restructuring complement other projects or initiatives in the business and how should it be managed alongside these?

Information systems strategy

Life in today's organisations is almost unrecognisable with the expansion of office technology and communications. Information systems strategies are demanding at a business, technical, cultural and especially political level. Therefore consider the following:

- Are all strategies aimed at changing information systems part of an overall information strategy which is, in turn, linked to both business strategy and intended organisational change?

- How have the cost/benefits of any information systems strategy been evaluated in terms of both internal and external benefits and costs, including:
  - customer value
  - access to markets
  - customer 'lock-in'
  - improving responsiveness
  - operational efficiency and capacity?

- Are changes in information systems seen as
  a) primarily of a technical issue; versus
  b) as also generating important and more difficult people-related and political issues? In the latter case, does the organisation have the necessary tools (like stakeholder analysis) and processes to gain maximum ownership for change?

- Who are the key stakeholders:
  a) of the end outputs of information systems; and
  b) as agents within the change process itself?

- Is there a risk of overrun against required timescales which might result in an expensive and disruptive 'crash programme' or a dilution of project benefits?

Management buy-out strategies

Management buy-outs may rank as one of the most difficult strategies which you may ever choose to contemplate undertaking. To help avoid this becoming Mission Impossible, consider the following:

- What are the main objectives of the buy-out project and to what extent are these shared by key management stakeholders? For instance:
    - freedom from head office *diktat.*
    - the possibility of making a significant capital gain.
    - protection of job security.
    - challenge of developing the business into new areas.
    - opportunity to renew the management team.

- Has the proposed management team the ability and balance to produce a quantum improvement in business performance or does it smack of 'more of the same'?

- What tangible changes will be made to support the symbolic event of the buy-out? For example, changing the company name, relocating premises, throwing out all the old stationery, reorganising managers' old office layouts, removing unnecessary status symbols; and how will these be project managed?

- Is there a robust strategy for improving the competitive position of the business or are the buy-out plans mainly aimed at producing 'the right set of numbers' to please venture capitalists? How will this strategy be project managed?

- Has the buy-out team got clear milestones for progress which are achievable but stretching?

- How will the issue of an 'exit route' to sell the business on (where this is applicable) be managed by the management team throughout the lifetime of the buy-out. (Are we managing the buy-out 'result' effectively?)

Alliance and joint venture strategies

We will give you checklists on acquisitions next.

Whilst acquisitions capture the headlines in the financial press, many organisations move their corporate strategy forward in a slightly more stealthily fashion through alliances (otherwise known as 'joint ventures'). A 'strategic alliance' can now be defined as:

"A longer-term strategic partnership between two or more organisations where there is investment in the venture by all of those partners, sharing both reward and risk."

Alliances may be thought of as being less risky than acquisitions. It is true that often the exposure of an alliance partner may be less (due to the sharing of risk and the fact that the commitment, although longer-term, is usually not quite so permanent). However, the riskiness of an alliance (sometimes known as a 'joint venture') can be higher due to:

- The very looseness of the arrangements.

- The need for a good deal of co-operation and openness.

- The fact that alliance partners may often have different aspirations (and possibly ones in tension or conflict), or different levels of bargaining power.

- The strategies of partners may change over time (and alongside that the personal agendas of key players in top management).

- The alliance itself will evolve and change as will its competitive environment.

Some key questions to reflect upon for any alliance (split up into the phases of formation and development) are as follows:

Formation

- What is the fundamental purpose of the alliance – what distinctive value does it add?

- Why is it likely to be better than other possible alliances?

- What are the different options for structuring and resourcing the alliance?

- To what extent is the alliance well-timed?

- How are the various needs and competencies of the alliance partners genuinely complementary?

- To what extent are these needs and competencies in tension or in potential conflict?

- To what extent is the alliance genuinely (therefore) a 'positive sum game' (or an arrangement where all parties are significantly better off through participating in the alliance)?

- What is the potential for the alliance leading on into a full acquisition, longer-term?

- Culturally, are the alliance partners likely to get on with each other: well, satisfactorily or, perhaps, badly?

- Have all partners got sufficient interest and commitment in the alliance to make it genuinely effective?

- Will an alliance with another partner(s) only give us a temporary advantage – as it will trigger other alliances in the industry?

- What are the potential risks and downsides to sustaining our core competencies by depending upon the alliance?

- Can we learn about how our partners do things really well and apply them elsewhere in our business without our partners becoming antagonistic?

- How long (realistically) do we think the alliance is likely to last?

- Who (if anyone) is likely to become the more dominant partner in the alliance, and if this is not likely to be us, what is the potential value of us being in the alliance?

- Do any arrangements for potential divorce adequately safeguard our interests?

- How will the formation of the alliance be project managed?

Development

- What investment is the alliance likely to require over time, and are alliance partners both able and willing to commit this when the time arrives?

- What senior management (and other scarce skills) is the alliance likely to need, and who will support this requirement?

- How will alliance partners conduct any reviews of performance and steer the strategy forward?

- In the event that the alliance takes off even more successfully than anticipated, how will it cope with this, particularly with regard to:
  - people;
  - structures;
  - financial resources.

- What processes for change of partners (including new ones coming in, old ones leaving or changes in partner stakes) be managed?

- How will alliance development be project managed (for example, what will its key milestones be)?

Setting strategy and objectives

Many acquisitions lack a robust strategy. To avoid this please ask the following:

- What is our own strategic position (i.e. of the acquirer), is it strong, average or weak?

- What strategic options (generally) for strategic development – alongside and including acquisition – do we have (including organic development, alliance, or buying-in the relevant skills directly)?

- Do we have the natural capabilities to screen and evaluate acquisitions (without getting carried away with the 'thrill of the chase') and also to negotiate a favourable deal and to integrate it effectively?

- Is this a good time for us to be thinking about acquisitions (for example, in terms of the economic cycle, competitive conditions and those of financial markets generally)?

- More specifically, what are our most important objectives for an acquisition project, and are these good or bad?

  'Good reasons' for making an acquisition might include:

  - Increasing our own shareholder value so we can add tangible value to the acquired business.

  - To acquire scarce capabilities (for example, management or technical skills) that we can apply elsewhere.

  - To build our own competitive advantage.

  'Bad reasons' for an acquisition project might include:

  - To grow the business (as an end in itself).

  - To enhance our own, personal careers.

  - Because we feel threatened by increased competition.

  - Because others are doing it, and we might get left behind.

- How will this phase be project managed?

Acquisition evaluation

Acquisition due diligence is often biased towards internal appraisal. To counter this please ask the following questions:

- How inherently attractive are the markets which our target is on (consider its growth drivers and the level of competitive pressure)?
- What is our target's underlying competitive position, and is it okay, average or weak?
- What is the basis of its competitive advantage, and is this likely to be sustainable given anticipated market and competitive change?
- How does it add distinctive value to its customers (if at all) and, if so, how does it capture this in the form of financial (and thus shareholder) value?
- How competitive is its cost base (and as against existing players and new entrants and/or distribution channels)?
- Are any of its products or markets moving into maturity or decline (life-cycle effects)?
- What is the strength of its management?
- How vulnerable is it likely to be to key staff leaving?
- Given our integration plans, how difficult (and uncertain) is integration likely to be?
- Where does the business currently make most/least money, and where does it destroy shareholder value (at the present time)?
- Where is the business likely to make most/least money in the future?
- What can we (genuinely) bring to the party in the way of value-added to the acquisition?
- How will this phase be project managed?

Negotiating the deal

The deal is the most important phase of the acquisition – and one which may be poorly handled by the inexperienced. Consider the following:

- Do we have a strong and experienced acquisition team – especially in terms of due diligence skills and negotiation skills?

- Will the team work well with each other – and avoid getting carried away with the 'thrill of the chase'?

- What competition might exist for the deal, and is this likely to push up the price to a level at which we become indifferent as to whether to go ahead or not with the deal?

- What is the relative balance in the bargaining power between buyer and seller – what is the relative pressure to buy or sell, and who has the most options?

- How skilled is the vendor's team in negotiating – and where are their likely vulnerabilities and weaknesses?

- Are we absolutely clear as to what we are bringing to the party versus what value is already inherent in the acquisition (so we avoid, in effect, paying twice)?

- Are there in-built check-points within the deal-making process for whether we carry on or not?

- Who will have the ultimate say over what we are prepared to offer?

Integration

Integration is an activity where strategic management will pay off in a very big way. Please consider the following questions:

- What key synergies are anticipated to be harvested through the acquisition?
- What changes are required in order to achieve these synergies – to products, services, operations, systems and processes, structures and people?
- Who are the key people who are essential both to protect and develop the business?
- How can they be convinced that it is worth backing the organisation following this period of pronounced uncertainty associated with the acquisition? For example through:
  - Selling the benefits of the acquisition in terms of future opportunity for their own development and reward.
  - Providing them with a clear role in integration and further development.
  - Spelling out openly the criteria for success and failure.
  - Protecting their self-respect through active incorporation of 'core best practices' into a new paradigm.
  - Having a clear and well communicated strategy for steering change.
- Is it planned to announce changes in leadership and structure quickly as opposed to playing a 'wait-and-see' game with the result of mounting uncertainty?
- Will changes in systems and control routines be handled with delicacy and sensitivity, and will sensible timescales be set to make changes? Where systems and control changes are required from 'day one' are there arrangements to support this externally?

- How will the issue of any culture change be handled, especially where it is intended to integrate a large part of operations? Does this reflect any pre-acquisition diagnosis of the key differences in culture between both organisations?

- How will learning about the acquisition be secured in terms both of 'what we have got for our money' (both internal and eternal capability) and also on the effectiveness of integration process?

- How will the phase of integration be project managed as a whole?

Operational strategies

Besides the more purely 'strategic' projects including organic development, acquisitions and alliances, there may also be some major operational projects. These can be grouped (for convenience) under the two main headings of:

- Operations expansion.
- Cost management and efficiency.

Operations expansion

- Based on the checklists dealing with selling more to existing customers/selling to new customers, etc (from 'Organic Development'), what is the potential for relatively easy-to-do expansion?

- To what extent can capacity be increased:
    - by physical expansion?
    - without physical expansion (and by the 'cunning plan')?
    - by appropriate out-sourcing?

- What productivity targets (by each and every incremental resource) need to be established?

- How will expansion be project managed?

Cost management and efficiency

- How cost-competitive are we against our existing competitors (now)?

- How cost-competitive are we against any new entrants (now)?

- How cost competitive are we likely to be (on current plans) vis-a-vis existing competitors and potential entrants?

- What are the key cost drivers within our current operational set-up and how can these be:

  a) incrementally improved;

  b) radically challenged (for example with zero-based approaches, i.e. working up from a situation of nil resources)?

- What are the key value drivers of the business and how can incremental value be added (and harvested) from a lower, or equivalent, or (preferably) a changed cost base?

- How can key business processes be re-engineered and simplified to make operations more efficient?

- Which other companies should we bench-mare and learn from – either from inside or outside the industry – to become more efficient?

- By customer bench-marking are there areas of activity that add little real customer value that we can reduce?

- How might cost management and efficiency initiatives be project managed?

Conclusion

The above strategies can be used both as checklists and also as suggested questions to help structure strategic workshops.

SEVEN
Conclusion – gurus and the future

The last couple of decades have been a fertile market for the strategy gurus. Most of these gurus have (especially the major ones) come from the US, and an even higher proportion from Harvard.

Only a handful of European (and even fewer UK thinkers) can really make pretence of having guru status. The Harvard Centre of gravity for gurus does seem to be almost self-perpetuating. Indeed, when the author himself sent a well-researched article to the Harvard Business Review he got only an impolite, standard letter, saying that only a few submissions were ever even looked at. (This is wildly at odds with the practise of other strategic management journals.) The author could not help suspect that you had to know someone 'on the inside' (i.e. the editorial board) even to get someone to take a quick look at it.

No doubt there are many extremely good and insightful ideas emanating from other non-US business schools, and consultants. And how often did we ever see MANAGERS writing in the Harvard Business Review? Virtually never, which seems very odd.

So probably, Harvard Business Review will continue to be populated by the type of gurus which we have covered in this book – with little fresh blood, and also relatively little international diversity.

This may be one of the factors which accounts for the lack in part of new ideas in the strategy industry, particularly over the last five to ten years (apart from Hamel and Prahalad and one or two others).

So where might the new ideas come from? What we sadly need is some new, revitalised form of Competitive Strategy, one which is no longer trapped in traditional, industry, corporate and business boundaries?

Perhaps a first step would be to simply imagine working with amnesia, having forgotten the Strategy Gurus completely, but having knowledge of all the other functional disciplines. Would anything be really missing from the world, what would have to be reinvented, and what might turn out to be quite different, and new?

Let me speculate for a moment.... we would obviously need to think about the future, and how we might manage it, so we might well find a need for FUTURE MANAGEMENT.

As a practical start in this I propose a new form of strategy, or CONTINGENT STRATEGY, which is defined as:

> *"An intended strategy which will be triggered on future conditions of alignment."*

The logic behind Contingent Strategy is that it would be folly to implement a strategy unless the world was aligned (at the time), to its success. As many strategies are fraught with uncertainty it only seems sensible to manage any commitment.

Hopefully this single form of strategy will provide a clue to Future Management.

I will leave the reader to ponder this...

Tony Grundy
2003

CONTACT DETAILS
Email: a.grundy@cranfield.ac.uk

Telephone: (44) 1494 873934

References

Ansoff, H I, *Corporate Strategy*, McGraw Hill, New York, 1965

Ansoff, *Managing Strategic Surprise by Response to Weak Signals*, Californian Management Review, XVIII, Winter 1975, pp 21-23

Argyris, C, *Strategy, Change and Defensive Routines*, Pitman, London, 1985

Argyris, C, *Teaching Smart People How to Learn*, Harvard Business Review, May-June 1991

Bartlett, C A and Ghoshal, S, *Managing Across Borders*, Harvard Business School Press, Harvard, 1989

Bennett Stewart II, G, EVA – *The Question for Value*, Harperbusiness, New York, 1991

Bowman, C, *The Essence of Competitive Strategy*, Prentice Hall, Hemel Hempstead 1985

Braybrooke, D and Lindblom, C E, *A Strategy of Decision*, Free Press, Macmillan, New York, 1963

Campbell and Goold, *Strategies and Styles*, Basil Blackwall, Oxford, 1987

Campbell, M, Goold M and Alexander M, *Corporate Level Strategy*, J Wiley & Son, New York, 1994

Chandler, A, *Strategy and Structure*, MIT Press, Mass, 1962

De Geus, A, *Planning as Learning*, Harvard Business Review, March-April, pp70-78, 1988

Goldratt, E, *Theory of Constraints*, North River Press, Great Barrington, Mass, 1990

Grant, R, *The Research-Based Theory of Competitive Advantage. The Implications for Strategy Formulation*, California Management Review, p14-35, Spring 1991

Grundy, A N, *Corporate Strategies and Financial Decisions*, Kogan Page, London, 1992

Grundy, A N, *Implementing Strategic Change*, Kogan Page, London, 1992

Grundy, A N, *Strategic Learning in Action*, McGraw Hill, Maidenhead

Grundy, A N, *Breakthrough Strategies for Growth*, Pitman Publishing, London, 1994

Grundy, A N., *Exploring Strategic Financial Management*, Prentice Hall, 1998b

Grundy, A N, *Harnessing Strategic Behaviour*, F T Publishing, London, 1998

Grundy, A N and Brown, L, *Strategic Project Management*, Thomson Learning, London, 2002

Grundy, A N, *Acquisitions and Mergers*, Capstone Publishing, Oxford, 2002b

Grundy, A N and Brown, L, *Be Your Own Strategy Consultant*, Thomson Learning, London, 2002

Grundy, A N, *Growth*, Capstone Publishing, Oxford, 2002d

Grundy, A N, *Shareholder Value*, Capstone Publishing, Oxford, 2002e

Grundy, A N and Brown, L, *Value-Based HR Strategy*, Butterworth Heinnemann, Oxford, 2003 (forthcoming)

Hamel, G and Prahalad, C K, *The Core Competence of the Organisation*, Harvard Business Review 68, No 3, pp 79-91, 1990

Hamel, G and Prahalad, C K, *Strategic Intent. Strategy as Stretch and Learning Leverage*, Harvard Business Review 67, No 3, p 63-76, 1989

Hamel, G and Prahalad, C K, *Strategy as Stretch and Learning*, Harvard Business Review 71, No 2, p 75-84, 1993

Hamel, G and Prahalad, C K, *Competing for the Future*, Harvard Business School Press, Boston, 1994

Handy, C, *Understanding Organisations*, Penguin, London 1976

Handy, C, *The Age of Unreason*, Business Book, Arrow, London, 1989

Handy, C, *The Empty Raincoat*, Hutchinson, London, 1994

Haspeslagh, P C and Jemison, D B, *Managing Acquisitions*, The Free Press, Macmillan, New York, 1991

Johnson, G and Scholes, *Exploring Corporate Strategy*, Prentice Hall, Hemel Hempstead, 1987

Kanter, R M, *The Change Masters*, Allen and Unwin, London, 1983

Kanter, R M, *When Giants Learn to Dance*, Simon & Schuster, New York, 1989

Kaplan and Norton, *The Balanced Score Card – Measures that Drive Performance*, Harvard Business Review, pp71-90, January-February 1992

Lewin, K. *A Dynamic Theory of the Personality*, McGraw Hill, New York, 1935

Lorange, P and Roos, J, *Strategic Alliances*, Blackwell, Cambridge, Mass, 1992

McTaggart, J M, Kontes, P W and Mankins, M C, *The Value Imperative*, The Free Press, Macmillan, New York, 1994

Milne, A A, *Winnie The Pooh*, The Metheun, 1926

Mintzberg, H, *The Nature of Management Work*, Harper and Row, New York, 1973

Mintzberg, H, *The Structuring of Organisations*, Prentice Hall, 1979

Mintzberg, H, *The Rise and Fall of Strategic Planning*, Prentice Hall, London, 1994

Mintzberg, H, Ahlstrand, B and Lampel, J, *Strategy Safari*, The Free Press, New York, 1998

Mitroff, I I and Linstome, H A, *The Unbounded Mind*, Oxford University Press, 1993

Ohmae, K, *The Mind of the Strategist*, McGraw Hill, New York, 1982

Pascale, R T and Athos, A, *The Art of Japanese Management*, Simon and Schuster, New York, 1981

Pascale, R T and Peters, T, *Managing on the Edge*, Simon and Schuster, New York, 1990

Peters, T, *In Search of Excellence* (with Waterman), Harper and Row, New York, 1982

Peters, T, *Thriving on Chaos*, Macmillan, London, 1987

Piercy, N, *Diagnosing and Solving Implementation Problems in Strategic Planning*, Journal of General Management, 15(1), pp 19-38, Autumn 1989

Porter, M E, *Competitive Strategy*, The Free Press, Macmillan, New York, 1980

Porter, M E, *Competitive Advantage*, The Free Press, Macmillan, New York, 1985

Porter, M E, *From Competitive Advantage to Corporate Strategy*, Harvard Business Review, May-June 1987

Porter, M E, *Strategy and the Internet*, Harvard Business Review, March 2001

Quinn, J B, *Strategies for Change: Logical Incrementalism*, Richard D Irwin, Illinois, 1980

Rappaport, A, *Creating Shareholder Value*, Free Press, Macmillan, New York, 1986

Reimann, B, *Managing a Value – A Guide to Value-based Strategic Management*, Blackwell, Oxford, 1990

Senge, P, *The Fifth Discipline. The Art and Practice of the Learning Organisation*, Doubleday, New York, 1990

Slyvosky, A J, *Value Migration*, Harvard Business School Press, Harvard, 1996

Spender, J C, *Strategy Making In Business*, Unpublished PhD thesis, University of Mass, 1980

Stalk, E, *Competing Against Time*, Free Press, Macmillan, 1990

Sun Tzu, *The Art of War* (various publications – see your bookshop)

Ulrich, D and Lake, D, *Organizational Capability: Competing from the Inside-Out*, Wiley, New York, 1990

Wack, P, *Scenarios: Unchartered Waters Ahead*, Harvard Business Review, pp 73-89, Sept-Oct 1985

Welch, J, Jack: *Straight from the Gut*, Warner Inc, New York, 2001

Yip, E S, *Total Global Strategy*, Prentice Hall, Englewood Cliffs, 1992

Thorogood publishing

Thorogood publishes a wide range of books, reports, special briefings, psychometric tests and videos. Listed below is a selection of key titles.

Desktop Guides

The marketing strategy desktop guide	Norton Paley	£16.99
The sales manager's desktop guide	Mike Gale and Julian Clay	£16.99
The company director's desktop guide	David Martin	£16.99
The credit controller's desktop guide	Roger Mason	£16.99
The company secretary's desktop guide	Roger Mason	£16.99
The finance and accountancy desktop guide	Ralph Tiffin	£16.99
The commercial engineer's desktop guide	Tim Boyce	£16.99
The training manager's desktop guide	Eddie Davies	£16.99
The PR practitioner's desktop guide	Caroline Black	£16.99
Win new business – the desktop guide	Susan Croft	£16.99

Masters in Management

Mastering business planning and strategy	Paul Elkin	£19.99
Mastering financial management	Stephen Brookson	£19.99
Mastering leadership	Michael Williams	£19.99
Mastering marketing	Ian Ruskin-Brown	£22.00
Mastering negotiations	Eric Evans	£19.99

Mastering people management	Mark Thomas • £19.99
Mastering personal and interpersonal skills	Peter Haddon • £16.99
Mastering project management	Cathy Lake • £19.99

Business Action Pocketbooks

Edited by David Irwin

Building your business pocketbook	£10.99
Developing yourself and your staff pocketbook	£10.99
Finance and profitability pocketbook	£10.99
Managing and employing people pocketbook	£10.99
Sales and marketing pocketbook	£10.99
Managing projects and operations pocketbook	£9.99
Effective business communications pocketbook	£9.99
PR techniques that work	*Edited by Jim Dunn* • £9.99
Adair on leadership	*Edited by Neil Thomas* • £9.99

Other titles

The John Adair handbook of management and leadership	*Edited by Neil Thomas* • £29.95
The inside track to successful management	*Dr Gerald Kushel* • £16.95
The pension trustee's handbook (3rd edition)	*Robin Ellison* • £25
Boost your company's profits	*Barrie Pearson* • £12.99
Negotiate to succeed	*Julie Lewthwaite* • £12.99

The management tool kit	*Sultan Kermally* • £10.99
Working smarter	*Graham Roberts-Phelps* • £15.99
Test your management skills	*Michael Williams* • £12.99
The art of headless chicken management	
	Elly Brewer and Mark Edwards • £6.99
EMU challenge and change – the implications for business	
	John Atkin • £11.99
Everything you need for an NVQ in management	
	Julie Lewthwaite • £19.99
Customer relationship management	*Graham Roberts-Phelps* • £12.99
Time management and personal development	
	John Adair and Melanie Allen • £9.99
Sales management and organisation	*Peter Green* • £9.99
Telephone tactics	*Graham Roberts-Phelps* • £9.99
Companies don't succeed people do!	*Graham Roberts-Phelps* • £12.99
Inspiring leadership	*John Adair* • £24.99
The book of ME	*Barrie Pearson and Neil Thomas* • £24.99
The complete guide to debt recovery	*Roger Mason* • £12.99
Janner's speechmaker	*Greville Janner* • £12.99
Dynamic practice development	*Kim Tasso* • £29.99

Thorogood also has an extensive range of reports and special briefings which are written specifically for professionals wanting expert information.

For a full listing of all Thorogood publications, or to order any title, please call Thorogood Customer Services on 020 7749 4748 or fax on 020 7729 6110. Alternatively view our website at **www.thorogood.ws**.